THE NIGHT
COMETH:
Two Wealthy Evangelicals
Face the Nation

THE NIGHT COMETH:
Two Wealthy Evangelicals Face the Nation

Rebecca J. Winter

William Carey Library

533 HERMOSA STREET • SOUTH PASADENA, CALIF. 91030

Library of Congress Catalog Card Number 77-087594
International Standard Book Number 0-87808-429-0

Published by the William Carey Library
533 Hermosa Street
South Pasadena, Calif. 91030

PRINTED IN THE UNITED STATES OF AMERICA

It is the fashion of some contemporary historians to minimize the significance of moral factors in history; to conclude that regardless of such men as Woolman and Wilberforce, Livingstone, and Lincoln, slavery would have disappeared anyway; and indeed, that the errors of each generation of the past have been inexorably outmoded by the impersonal working of material forces. Such thinking is the vestigal remnant of a romanticism now sadly discredited, and its dangerous unreality has been made clear by contemporary experience. Nothing in human history promises that evil will ever be eliminated without toil, pain, and vicarious suffering, or without the inspiration of men animated by the noble insights of religion .

Ernest Marshall Howse

Contents

Foreword

In recent decades, evangelicals have been accused of a lack of concern about the physical and social needs of the world. Their enthusiasm for making disciples of all men has created an assumption that they are therefore uncommitted to meeting the total needs of man with the whole gospel.

History, of course, when told accurately, can show the opposite. It is precisely when men are born anew into God's kingdom and controlled by His Spirit that they are given the tremendous patience, love, commitment, and conscience necessary to struggle successfully against the massive problems confronting mankind.

The Night Cometh contains a prime example of two such men, unusually wealthy and unusually committed to God's cause on earth. God's people are called to be light and salt in the world; here is an account of two brothers who took that call seriously . . . two men who can speak to us, a century later, about our own response to that call.

Arthur DeMoss
Robert DeMoss

Preface

Evangelicals today struggle to define their responsibilities within the moral, physical, and spiritual needs of the world. How connected is evangelism to the needs of human societies? How far does Christ call us to go? Seemingly, we struggle alone to discover God's highest purpose for our individual and corporate lives. And yet . . .

Within the scattered strands of information preserved from the past, the far off echoes of God's powerful work among men can be reconstructed. Our distant perspective allows us to see more clearly the way God has transformed both individuals and societies through the consecrated lives of those wholly committed to him. The work of God's people in the past challenges us now towards a higher commitment to His work in the present.

Such is the impact of the lives of Lewis and Arthur Tappan — two wealthy evangelicals of the last century. The depth of their commitment to Christ, and the startling way God used that commitment to transform America, continues to challenge me to renewed dedication of my own walk with Christ. Recorded herein is the Tappans' participation as two of last century's radical evangelicals: Christians who had a deep (though often overlooked) impact on America and her people — because of their radical commitment to Christ.

The lives of Lewis and Arthur Tappan encompassed a wide spectrum, from the studied and wholehearted commitment of their enormous incomes, to a concern with minority rights and education, to church planting in New York City slums, the rehabilitation of outcasts, and a passionate involvement in the moral issues of the day. They were to have an amazing effect on the lives of friends, enemies, and America herself. If little is known about Lewis and Arthur Tappan today, it is not because they did little worthy of note.

The book was written as an historically accurate account. It was not intended to make a point or to persuade towards a particular conclusion, nor was it, in fact, originally intended for a wide audience. Nevertheless, it is hoped that the lives of the Tappan brothers will unfold for each reader as a challenge as well as an exciting factual account. No doubt, we all can learn both from their mistakes as well as their victories. Many of their own writings have been used in order to catch a glimpse of their internal struggles, prayers, and joys. From these few, almost forgotten, writings from the past it is hoped that each of us may catch a vision of God's call on our own lives, and respond prayerfully to His challenge to be His ambassadors to the world.

The astonishingly broad concern for society and the hearts of men was alive then and is alive now not only in America but around the world as missionaries have carried this full range of concern to the immense needs of foreign countries as well. Indeed, my own personal interest in this theme was more than anything else sparked by growing up in a foreign country where I could observe first hand how missionaries—and specifically my parents—were wrestling effectively with a wide range of problems fundamental to social and economic development.

Thus the Tappan's kind and quality of Christianity does live on as 37,000 American missionaries continue active amidst a vast international empire. They are incredibly more influential than the average person could imagine, as possibly every Tappan project is reflected a thousand times over in distant lands across the earth. Today, of course, a host of secular and governmental agencies have evolved to carry forward the schools, hospitals and technical institutes initiated by the missionary, but the source and ultimate solution is still the spiritual base and motivation which is so clearly inextricable in the lives of these two earlier disciples of Jesus Christ.

I would like to extend my sincerest thanks to the number of people who helped me produce this book: to Bradley Gill for his hard work to produce just the right cover, to Robert Coleman, Jr. for his long hours of editing, to Professor Bob Rosenstone at the California Institute of Technology for his helpful suggestions and experience in American history research, to Laurel Sherman for her hospitality during my stay in Washington, D.C. while I was studying manuscripts at the Library of Congress, to my father, Ralph D. Winter, whose historical research and teaching first lifted this period into my attention, and most of all to my mother, Mrs. Roberta Winter, for her tremendous help in researching and rewriting many sections of the book.

Rebecca J. Winter

1

The Critical Years

IT WAS 1836. Two brothers, both millionaires and both devout Christians, were under siege. Lewis had only a few weeks earlier completed his new home on Rose Street in a quiet, middle-class section of New York City. Now, late at night in his family's absence, a mob had converged, hacked his doors, furniture and pictures to pieces and burned them in a huge bonfire. Arthur's name, meanwhile, was being broadcast far and wide as a wanted man. Almost a million dollars in today's currency was offered for his deliverance, dead or alive, to a New Orleans address. And the owner of the store across the street from his importing company had also offered $150,000 to anyone who would kill him. Newspapers reviled them both, in issue after issue. Even the police turned their backs and ignored their danger. Arthur and Lewis must have felt utterly alone in their troubles.

Why would two men, so wealthy and so devout, absolutely infuriate so many people? That question begins a long story, almost totally forgotten in our day, and believable only if we go back briefly to 1792 to an America we may not recognize, a nation with a new dream and with seemingly impossible problems.

Washington, usually unperturbable, was alarmed. So was John Adams. It had been only a few short years since the Revolutionary War had been won, yet liberty had not brought the long sought peace. Like teenagers suddenly aware of their prowess, the newly independent Americans, now having no British authority to resist, resisted the newly established American one. They felt self-sufficient for any crisis and didn't want nor feel the need for any centralized leadership. Bad habits, useful in winning a war, proved irksome and even dangerous in establishing a nation. Privateers had hassled British shipping, and along with the merchants, had become quite adept at smuggling. Former soldiers, now farmers, had dulled consciences about the use of firearms against other human beings. The long war had developed ingenuity aplenty, and daring to match it. But close to the surface of the American temperament there was also a certain spirit that didn't want taming. "No taxation without representation" had been the rallying cry before the Revolution; taxation was still hated, even though the taxing government was here on this continent.

One source of the problem was economic. The war had been expensive, and the newly born government had huge debts. The Congress and the individual states together owed about $25,000,000 at the close of the war. There was a widespread and severe depression as a result, which lasted for about six years. Large numbers of people, unable to pay their debts with useless continental exchange, were jammed into debtor prisons where they thought hard thoughts about what they had fought to win. Others, led by Shay, attacked a government arsenal, and so alarmed Washington that he himself started for the "front" before the rebels were routed in a surprise attack by state militia. Writing to Madison on November 5, 1786, Washington expressed the fears of many of the founding fathers: "We are fast verging to anarchy and confusion!"[1]

But the problem was not merely economics. Washington's cabinet, composed of men highly respected then as now, was nevertheless a fractious, quarrelling mess. Hamilton, as Secretary of the Treasury, made a number of suggestions to help discharge the national debt, and Jefferson, as Secretary of State, rejected them all, heatedly. The debate turned into a public fracas, Jefferson calling Hamilton "the evil genius of America"[2] and Hamilton accusing Jefferson of "a womanish attachment to France and French ideals."[3]

By Jefferson's own account, he and Hamilton from the start were "pitted against each other every day in the cabinet like two fighting-cocks."[4] It is no wonder that Washington wondered "if any living man (could) manage the helm . . . or keep the machine together."[5]

It is true that Jefferson was enamored with France — especially after the French Revolution, and he showed this clearly when he donned the red breeches and waistcoat of that Revolution. To have a man so high in government so much in favor of a France that had gone to extremes frankly frightened all Federalists like Hamilton. Democracy they wanted, but a limited one. The "democracy" of the French Revolution — if it could be called that — had resulted in the execution of not only the king and queen but hundreds of the learned and aristocratic populace. Lafayette, of American fame, had barely escaped though he was known to have always held to semi-republican ideals. As a result, leading American politicians who had considered themselves liberal admitted regretfully to having been too republican in the past, and now believed the troubles of America to be the result of "an excess of democracy."[6] Timothy Dwight, Jonathan Edward's grandson and perhaps one of the greatest of Yale College presidents, feared that "the great object of democracy was to destroy every trace of civilization in the world and force mankind back into a savage state."[7] And Hamilton, when confronted with the idea of a government by the people, as in France, exploded "Your people, sir — your people is a great beast!"[8]

The republicanism of France seemed the more dangerous because French philosophy, on which it was based, had become the rage in American colleges and intellectual circles since before our war for independence. Voltaire, Rousseau, and D'Alambert were read so widely and admired so greatly that for some time students at Yale, Harvard and Princeton called each other by those names.[9] Agnosticism and infidelity were common, bolstered by the writings of our own revolutionary heroes Thomas Paine and Ethan Allen and loudly proclaimed by the many infidel clubs which were set up all over the nation.[10] Dwight deplored the situation and accused France, Germany and England of vomiting "the dregs of infidelity . . . upon this country."[11] His accusations were not without some foundation since anti-Christian Frenchmen had "subscribed three million francs to print and distribute books to influence the minds of young Americans."[12]

Religion was so ridiculed in the colleges that the one or two students who dared profess it found themselves not only the objects of scorn and ridicule but at times even in physical danger. At Hampden-Sydney (a Presbyterian school in Virginia) the president of the college, investigating an uproar, found a barricaded band of three who had met for prayer and invited them to use his private room lest they be harmed by the attacking rowdies.[13] Campuses were known as centers of cheating, profanity, lying, drunkenness, and immorality.[14]

The loss of moral conscience was not limited to the colleges. Philadelphia, the seat of government in 1798, although founded by pious Quakers was now in such a state of moral decay that a French emigre commented that

> Morals in this city . . . are not pure, although they pretend to be virtuous. When a Quakeress feels lecherous impulses, she notifies her husband of it, and does her best to make him share her torment. Quaker youths are frequent visitors in the houses of ill fame . . . The daughters of Quakers are extremely imprudent and frequently get into trouble. Bastards are extremely common.[15]

Frontiersmen were not so sophisticated as the collegians and the Philadelphians, and they tended to be not only irreligious but lawless, violent, and given to drunken rowdiness. Dwight spoke of those in the Maine frontier as "vicious men" while Lorenzo Dow said that the people of Western New York were "the off scouring of the earth."[16] Peter Cartwright, himself a product of the frontier, said that "the Kentucky of his boyhood in the seventeen-nineties, was the abode of 'murderers, horse thieves, highway robbers and counterfeiters.' "[17] The custom of eye gouging in fights was so common in the South, especially in Virginia and Kentucky, that one traveler said that "in Philadelphia it is imagined that one-quarter of the Virginians have lost their eyes by gouging . . ."[18]

Easy access to alcohol added to the problem. "Of a population of 5 million, the United States suffered 300,000 drunkards, and buried about 15,000 of them annually . . . drunkenness being indulged in to a frightening degree, to incredible excess."[19] It was commonplace for part of a workman's wages to be paid in hard liquor. Even churches followed this practice, and the liquor was so often distilled by the minister himself that in the 1830s the Methodist church (which had been dry at its inception) felt compelled to enjoin its ministers "not to distill or sell liquor."[20] Alcohol in one form or another was so common a drink that to drink only water set one down as a pauper "reduced to animal provender like the Prodigal with the swines' husks."[21] The famous newspaper editor, Horace

Greeley, estimated that a barrel of hard cider "hardly lasted a week in a family of 6 to 8."[22]

In our time we tend to think of the early days of our nation as being the days when righteousness prevailed, and the church was highly revered. That may have been true to some extent in the seventeenth century and after the great revivals of the first quarter of the nineteenth, and even for some years in the mid-eighteenth. But organized religion was met with a great deal of scorn during the revolutionary period until the close of that century.

In such a society, clergymen suffered much ridicule. Some of them blamed Jefferson for the state of affairs. Jefferson was well known as a deist. He had rewritten the gospels, omitting those passages which did not suit his philosophy, and thumbed his nose at the traditional institutional church. One writer says that "Jefferson vied with Paine for the role of the best-hated man among conservative Christians,"[23] and on at least one occasion a Virgianian senator complained that at Jefferson's dinner table in a discussion of religion only a Jew would join him in a defense of the character of Jesus.[24]

When Jefferson insisted that the state and the church be separated in the government of this country, religious leaders like Lyman Beecher, father of Harriet Beecher Stowe, were sure that Christianity would go into total eclipse. And perhaps his fears were well founded. In Virginia in 1818 one visitor complained that "the ancient Episcopal churches which once were so predominant, are mostly in a state of dilapidation. The rank reeds rustle round their doors; the fox looks out at their windows."[25] Because of its loyalist sympathies during the war, the Episcopal church had lost most of its clergy and much of its membership. Methodist parishes had likewise suffered, especially in the northern colonies, again because of their close connection to an English church.

In New England and the Middle Colonies, church membership losses were due more to an infatuation with French philosophy than to loyalist emigration or abandonment. In these two areas the revivals of the 1740s had had their greatest effect, but the war had destroyed some of the churches, many of the manses, and in short (in the words of a tune popular at the time) had turned the world upside down for Americans as well as for British.

For some time the state of religion in the South had been deplorable. The ministers had been so given to drunkenness and gambling that the Rev. Jonathan Boucher called many of the Anglican ministers in Maryland "a despicable class" and "shabby

Christians" and wondered seriously if enemies of Protestantism in England had not been responsible for the assignment of such dissolute ministers to Anglican pulpits in America.[26] It was little wonder, then, that Sundays in the Carolinas were considered days of "riot and drunkenness."[27] Jefferson's disenchantment with the church is better understood when we read the diary of one visitor to South Carolina:

> In South Carolina, cards, dice and the bottle and horses engross prodigious proportions of the time . . . The Sabbath is a day of visiting and mirth with the rich, of license, pastime and folly with the negroes . . . quarreling round the doors of the churches in service-time, while their masters in the pews withindoors chatted socially during the sermon perfunctorily preached from the pulpit."[28]

When this same early visitor wrote about the "depravity and abominable wickedness" of the clergy in that area, his recitation of the local gossip about the minister was so lurid that "some later hand tore out the two diary pages following Quincey's mention of parsons neglecting their parishes to run taverns and gamble."[29] All too commonly it was recorded of such ministers: "The Parson is drunk and can't perform the duties of his office."[30] One fought a duel in the churchyard; another married a wealthy widow in America even though he already had a wife back in England.[31]

With their Puritan background, New Englanders had greater respect for their ministers, but as wealth increased, interest in a more formal high-church type of service and a reaction against revivalistic enthusiasm set in. Thus the new rationalism of Locke with its emphasis on man's natural goodness had a genuine appeal, and Congregationalists in particular were so attracted that eventually the Unitarian movement within the church became a separate denomination.

The state of religion in the Middle States was also so deplorable that the General Assembly of the Presbyterian Church in 1798 condemned the "profaneness, pride, luxury, injustice, intemperance, lewdness, and every species of debauchery and loose indulgence" which were all too common.[32]

The war had been the watershed. In the 1740s, Jonathan Edwards in New England and Gilbert Tennent in New Jersey had spearheaded a revival movement which eventually swept over most of the colonies, receiving assistance from George Whitfield in Georgia and Pennsylvania. By 1765 the revival excitement had died down to be replaced by a very real excitement for war with England.

Revival pastors were almost always pro-independence, and urged participation in the hostilities. Yet

> The effects of war on the churches of all communions were extensively and variously disastrous. To say nothing of the distraction of the mind from the subject of salvation, its more palpable influences were seen and felt everywhere. Young men were called away from the seclusion and protection of the paternal roof, and from the vicinity of the oracle of God, to the demoralising atmosphere of a camp; congregations were sometimes entirely broken up; churches were burnt, or converted into barracks or hospitals, by one or other of the belligerent armies; often by both successively; in more than one instance pastors were murdered; the usual ministerial intercourse was interrupted; efforts for the dissemination of the gospel were, in a great measure, suspended; colleges and other seminaries of learning were closed for want of students and professors; and the public morals in various respects, and in almost all possible ways, deteriorated. Christianity is a religion of peace, and the tempest of war never fails to blast and scatter the leaves of the tree which was planted for the healing of the nations.[33]

Whether it was caused by the war or not, one aspect of the American personality which always amazed foreigners who visited during this period of time was their cruelty. Slavery in the South provided an opportunity for cruelty to the negro, but it was not in the South that one horrified visitor watched as a seemingly respectable crowd with feelings ranging from indifference to enthusiasm witnessed the burning alive of a colored man.[34] They were equally enthusiastically attracted to public hangings. Perhaps we should not wonder, then, at the violence that erupted in personal duels, even between men of such stature as Vice President Aaron Burr and Alexander Hamilton, resulting in the latter's death, or clubbings on the floor of the Senate, or the "stabbing, shooting, gouging out of eyes, biting off of noses or ears (which) were not uncommon."[35] Foreign visitors half expected frontiersmen to be rough and cruel, but they were shocked to see how prone respectable men were to "throw themselves savagely on someone who had inadvertently provoked them."[36] Even though dueling was technically illegal everywhere in the States, it was quite common, especially in the South. This can be attested to by the number of tombstones bearing the words "killed on the field of honor", by the scores of highly placed men who had dueling scars (Andrew Jackson boasted openly of his),[37] and by "the fact that a book called *The Code of Honor, or Rules for the Government of Principals and Seconds in Duelling,* written by a governor of South Carolina, was reprinted regularly until as late as 1858."[38]

Nor can this cruelty be blamed on codes of behavior brought over from the old country, even though duelling was still practiced into the 20th century in Germany. Immigrants did, however, affect American life. Ours has always been a country of immigrants, but with the French Revolution and the potato famine in Ireland, they flocked by the thousands to the States in the last quarter of the eighteenth century, particularly to the North where there was a market for cheap white labor. The Irish in particular were violently anti-British just at a time when the Federalists (as opposed to the French loving Republicans) were striving to cement a friendly relationship with England. The result was a series of Federalist inspired Alien and Sedition Acts which infuriated Jefferson and his cohorts and started our first major anti-alien scare. To the Yankees, the Irish seemed dirty, drunken, rowdy and lazy — in short, totally undesirable as new citizens. The best hope one clergyman could offer was that they would probably die early and thus become extinct.[39] Germans and British joined the Irish and French, often being fleeced by "immigrant runners" before they ever left the slums by the harbor for their more permanent abodes. Immigrant girls were lured into houses of "ill repute" which became so common in New York that one young man complained in 1830 that "It's a pity we've no street but Broadway that's fit to walk in of an evening. The street is always crowded, and whores and blackguards make up about two-thirds of the throng."[40] Even Boston, with its Puritan origins, had its "houses of ill fame (which) were kept 'without concealment and without shame.' "[41] There was no more sense of unity among the differing immigrant groups battling for space than there was during the racial riots of the twentieth century. Policemen then as later in American history hesitated to interfere in the local battles between Irish gangs and German gangs which were called such names as the "Pug Uglies, the Forty Thieves, the Swamp Angels, the Slaughterhouse Boys."[42]

America in 1800 was a new nation — reckless, impatient, headlong, untamed. It was a nation on the move, the wagons pouring through the Cumberland gap numbering in the hundreds. It was a nation with a dream which encompassed the entire continent. And it was a nation in social and moral turmoil.

> While religion was deeply stamped on colonial institutions and minds, few bothered to be observant. Later Americans would often

be supplied a mythology which paraded the founding fathers as intensely Christian men. Citizens were often told that there had been a great fall from a golden age when those who formed the nation had all believed and worshipped passionately. Just the opposite was the case. At no other moment in the two hundred years of national experience were religious institutions so weak as they were in the first quarter-century after independence. It is difficult to establish reliable statistics, but the best guesses suggest that from four to seven per cent of the people were formally church members — about one tenth as large a figure as twentieth-century America saw.[43]

Then something happened. Between 1800 and 1850 America changed, drastically — so drastically that Alexis de Toqueville spoke of the religion which more than any nation he had ever visited permeated all of American life. What the America of 1800 not only tolerated but enjoyed, it repudiated at great cost and bloodshed in 1860. Laws were rewritten. Public sentiment turned a corner.

The change began almost simultaneously in the frontier (Kentucky and Tennessee), in the South (at Hampden-Sydney and Washington Colleges in Virginia), and in the Northeast (at Yale and in Boston). Looking perhaps to the Committees of Correspondence that had unified the colonies to prepare for war, and more recently to the Concert of Prayer that was sweeping England,[44] Christian businessmen and ministers suggested in 1794 that a "Concert of Prayer" be "addressed to ministers and churches of every known denomination in all the United States" suggesting that united prayer be made for a spiritual awakening that would change the nation.[45] Response was not all-encompassing, but it spanned different denominational and social barriers, literally turning Yale College around and making it in a few short years a center from which missionaries would be sent around the globe. Rolls of the churches in different areas show sudden leaps in membership, depending on precisely when the awakening in that area began.

In Massachusetts about this time two boys were born two years apart into a pious household. Their names were never to become household words, not widely known even to later historians, but they were to become very wealthy and highly influential in their own generation. Neither was more than a wealthy good man until touched by the awakening which resulted from this Concert of Prayer.

NOTES

1. Morris, Richard B. and the Editors of *Life, The Making of a Nation,* Volume 2 of *The Life History of the United States.* New York: Time, Inc., 1963, p. 113.

2. Coit, Margaret L. and the Editors of *Life*, *The Growing Years*, Vol. 3 of *The Life History of the United States*. New York: Time, Inc., 1963, p. 10.

3. Ibid., p. 15.

4. Loc. cit.

5. Ketchum, Richard M., *The World of George Washington* New York: The American Heritage Publishing Company, 1974, p. 191.

6. Tyler, Alice Felt, *Freedom's Ferment, Phases of American Social History from the Colonial Period to the Outbreak of the Civil War*. New York: Harper & Row, 1944, p. 12.

7. Loc. cit.

8. Loc. cit.

9. Marsden, George M., *The Evangelical Mind and the New School Presbyterian Experience: A Case Study of Thought and Theology in Nineteenth-Century America*. New Haven: Yale University Press, 1970, p. 9.

10. Orr, J. Edwin, *The Eager Feet: Evangelical Awakenings, 1790-1830*. Chicago: Moody Press, 1975, p. 11.

11. Ibid., p. 9.

12. Loc. cit.

13. Ibid., p. 66.

14. Ibid., p. 9.

15. Cable, Mary and the Editors of American Heritage, *American Manners & Morals*. New York: American Heritage Publishing Co., Inc., 1969, p. 91.

16. Weisberger, Bernard A., *They Gathered at the River: The Story of the Great Revivalists and Their Impact Upon Religion in America*. Boston: Little, Brown and Company, 1958, p. 11.

17. Loc. cit.

18. Furnas, J.C., *The Americans: A Social History of the United States, 1587-1914*. New York: G.P. Putnam's Sons, 1969, p. 182.

19. Orr, Op. cit. p. 8.

20. Cable, Op. cit., p. 90.

21. Furnas, Op. cit., p. 142.

22. Ibid., p. 143.

23. Weisberger, Op. cit., p. 7.

24. Loc. cit.

25. Cable, Op. cit., p. 89.

26. Furnas, Op. cit., pp. 184-5.

27. Weisberger, Op. cit., p. 7.

28. Furnas, Op. cit., p. 183.

29. Loc. cit.

30. Ibid., p. 184.

31. Loc. cit.

32. Orr, Op. cit., p. 11.

33. Baird, Robert, *Religion in the United States of America*. New York: Arno Press & the New York Times, 1969, p. 222.

34. Pessen, Edward, *Jacksonian America: Society, Personality, and Politics*. Homewood, Illinois: The Dorsey Press, 1969, p. 14.

35. Ibid., p. 15.

36. Loc. cit.

37. Cable, Op. cit., p. 97.

38. Ibid., p. 95.

39. Ibid., p. 99.

40. Pessen, Op. cit., p. 67.

41. Loc. cit.

42. Loc. cit.

43. Marty, Martin E., *Righteous Empire: The Protestant Experience in America.* New York: The Dial Press, 1970, p. 38.

44. Orr, Op. cit., p. 191.

45. For a much more extensive discussion, see chapters 7, 8, 9, 11, 17, and 19 of Orr, Op. cit.

2

The Influence of Sarah Tappan

ARTHUR TAPPAN was born at Northampton, Massachusetts, on May 22, 1786. He was the eighth child, and fifth son of Benjamin and Sarah Tappan, in a family of eleven children, nine of which survived. Lewis Tappan, the next child, was born two years later on May 26, 1788. There were six surviving Tappan sons — Benjamin, Jr., William, Charles, John, Arthur, and Lewis — who were to continue to interact with each other throughout their life times.

The most consistent influence on the early lives of Lewis and Arthur Tappan was their mother, Sarah Tappan. Their father, Benjamin Tappan, was a minister's son, strict but not severe, and his good humor and upright morals provided an example that his children were not to forget. However, as Lewis Tappan points out in his biography of Arthur, while they "reverenced" their father, all of the children had "a most affectionate regard" for their mother.[1] The closeness they felt toward her was a natural result of the deep and unflagging concern that she demonstrated for them as individuals, with a combination of strict instruction, correction, and warm affection.

From their earliest remembrance, Lewis and Arthur were exposed to her consistent and determined instruction, both verbal and non-verbal. The message was clear to them — though "it was her endeavor to gratify her children so far as would be for their good, . . . it was her especial desire to be faithful to their souls."[2] So great was her concern for the spiritual growth and well-being of her children that after they left home, and even when they were well into their middle-age, she filled her letters with theological debates, exhortation, Biblical instruction, the workings of God in her own life, and prayers for the son or daughter to whom she was writing.

When they were young she kept a strict vigil over their actions on the Sabbath. She taught them hymns and portions of the "Westminster Assembly's Catechism" which they later would recite to their father. Playing outside or making noise was forbidden; reading of religious materials or good books was encouraged, but few of the latter were available and neither were well adapted to the taste and capacity of young people. Lewis Tappan recalls the Sabbath of his childhood as being overly austere. He mentions only two redeeming features — they were never whipped on the Sabbath and, after the "catechising" their mother would always bring forth a delicious oblong apple pie to be distributed among the children, those who had studied most diligently being rewarded with the corner piece. Lewis notes, however, that in later age even his mother came to realize the undue strictness she had maintained on the Sabbath, regretting that she had not allowed them greater indulgence — at least in the type of books they were allowed to read.[3]

But Sarah Tappan's children realized that she was not strict with them out of a spirit of bitterness, anger, or a desire to dominate, but rather out of love. They saw that she did not require anything of them that she did not also require of herself. In many instances, her devotion to God caused her to be even stricter with herself than she ever was with others. The source of her single-minded concern with the things of God she herself attributed to her conversion, through the work of the Holy Spirit, at the age of twenty. As she explained in a letter to her sons Charles and Lewis, written in March 1824, her faith was not

> the effect of an early education . . . as Lewis and yourself [Charles] seem to think. My parents, it is true, were orthodox in sentiment and truly pious, but if they endeavored to make me either, it was a lost labour, at least until I was nearly twenty years old. So far, that I was then without any knowledge of God, or the way of salvation by

redemption offered in his word; not but that I had experienced the strivings of the Holy Spirit and had made repeatedly what I called good resolutions, which were soon forgotten . . . I heard a plain sermon from these words, "What shall it profit a man tho' he gain the whole world and lose his own soul." I recollected I had often heard sermons from that text, but never felt the truth as it was enforced. The impression was deep and lasting . . . From this time, without anyone to assist me, the truths contained in the Bible opened more fully to my mind, and I read and heard with a great astonishment at my past wilful (sic) ignorance. I was indeed as one new born, and God's glorious character was visible in all his works to that degree that I thought it wonderful the stones did not upbraid man with his ingratitude, for all else that had breath or life seemed to utter forth his praise . . . And through many temptations and much weakness, I have been enabled to preservire (sic) and to receive light more abundantly. I am waiting in hope for my great change, when I shall be freed from sin, and prayer shall cease to be a delightful privilege, all, all, shall be turned to praise . . . but here my heart must have continued sorrow for those who *will* not believe.[4]

This experience did indeed make a "deep and lasting" impression on Sarah Tappan, as this letter was written when she was seventy-six years old, just two years before her death in 1826. The tone of the letter also serves to express, in many ways, the tone of her life. In her mind, Biblical training was not enough to gain a knowledge of God and of salvation — this fact she had seen in her own life. She wrote this letter to Charles and Lewis as a final effort to reinforce once more in their minds their need for an "entire change of heart and pursuits; that you may love God supremely, and place your chief happiness in obeying his precepts."[5] A moral life, good deeds, church attendance, and knowledge of the Scriptures is not enough, she continually emphasized, for a knowledge of God or for salvation. Yet God is not distant and hard to approach, she maintained: "We have abundant reason to believe that if we are sincere in seeking for mercy, we shall have God on our side. If God was not more willing to save us than we are to be saved, he never would have given up his Son a ransom for sinners, nor informed us of it in his word, nor sent the Holy Spirit to convince us of sin, and urge us to repentance."[6]

So also she expressed the faith that she had in the ability of the Bible, with the aid of the Holy Spirit, to open the mind of any sincere, concerned reader to the truth of God's message and His way of salvation. "But the word of God is plain," she told Arthur. "Study it attentively, with sincere and fervent prayer for the outpouring of the Holy Spirit to enlighten your darkened understanding, and make your path of duty plain. God is a prayer-hearing God. He has not said to the seed of Jacob, seek my face in vain."[7]

Sarah Tappan did truly sorrow for those who continued to refuse to believe — especially her own children. Despite her continual admonitions, however, Arthur did not understand the significance of her entreaties until he himself experienced a "new birth" in his thirties (early in the 1820's). Lewis, in describing Arthur's seven years of apprenticeship from age fifteen to twenty, comments: "It is not intended that, at this time, he had experienced the regenerating grace of God. The instructions and prayers of his parents, and the other religious teachings in his boyhood, though they had some effect upon his conscience, had not induced him to secure 'the pearl of great price'. And the religious teachings during the after years of his minority had influenced him to think a change of heart was unnecessary, that a good moral character was about all that was required."[8]

Likewise, Sarah's counsels and instructions served merely to convince Lewis only of the necessity of remaining true to that which he felt the Bible taught doctrinally. He was frustrated by his mother's conviction that he had not yet really encountered God, as she insinuated in her letter in 1824. He was surprised when almost two years after her death, he himself experienced an "entire change of heart" at age 39. Such an experience was the last thing he expected — he had found something which he had always thought he already had, only to discover that it was completely different than anything he had previously conceived it to be.

From what has been said, it might be easy to get the impression that Sarah Tappan displayed an almost overly-pious, self-righteous, or judgmental attitude with respect to the faith and beliefs of others. However, this interpretation of her concern is not consistent with her sincere conviction of her own worthlessness apart from God. She wrote Arthur, saying,

> I feel that I am depraved in the whole man; that in me naturally there is no good; that all my sufficiency is of God; and it is my happiness that I may go to him as a guilty, weak and helpless creature, and cast all my cares on him. He has promised never to leave me or forsake me, and I can trust his word. It is this comfort, my dear child, I wish you to enjoy. It is what the world can neither give, nor deprive us of.[9]

The Tappans lived in Northampton, Massachusetts, the town in which Jonathan Edwards had had his greatest impact and ministry.

In fact, the Tappans lived in the old Edwards home for a number of years.[10] Sarah Tappan herself was converted in 1768 in the same general revival movement started by Jonathan Edwards and George Whitfield, an evangelist from England. Whitfield's renowned voice and exceptional speaking powers amazed even Benjamin Franklin, who refused to carry any money when going to hear him speak because, no matter what his previous resolve, he always ended up "emptying my pockets." Franklin calculated once that Whitfield's voice was sufficient to speak to over 30,000 people unaided. Sarah Tappan, also, was impressed by his teaching, and would often go over his sermons with her children.[11]

To Sarah, her children's moral character was an integral part of their spiritual training. By example and instruction, she left a definite impression on their minds of the importance of generosity and service. After her death, Lewis reminisced:

> If she had any luxury she was sure to impart it to the sick. Her children always knew that if they sent their mother any good thing, oranges for example when they were rare, their mother would view the risk of their decaying in order to keep them for some sick neighbor. When a child, she would often send us to the next house, to an old mansion, now removed, with broth or something wholesome, to an old lady named King. And the influence upon the hearts of children, in sending them on such errands, is very beneficial . . . often did she remark that she would prefer having her children sincere Christians to being the richest and most honored of the world.[12]

Sarah did not stop at personal example and instruction, but sought also to expand the perspectives and concerns of her children by keeping them informed about the great reforming efforts of others, for example, those of Wilberforce and the "Clapham Sect" in England.* The awareness she instilled in her children was a foreshadow of Lewis and Arthur's later involvement as great reform leaders themselves.

When Arthur first and then Lewis left home, three years apart at age fifteen, to begin their training and work in Boston, the input they received from their mother naturally decreased. An occasional letter, and even less frequent visits, were not sufficient to prevent them from drifting from their mother's beliefs and hopes. It would

---

*The Clapham Sect was a powerfully motivated group of men (some in Parliament) who for the most part resided in the town of Clapham in England. They were products of the Evangelical Awakening, and like the Tappans in America, were motivated by their Christian zeal to all sorts of reform.

be more than fifteen years before they would be in accord with her views or experience the "change of heart" she hoped and prayed that they would have.

NOTES

1. Lewis Tappan, *The Life of Arthur Tappan* (Westport, Conn., 1970), 16.
2. Ibid., 17.
3. Ibid., 24.
4. Sarah Tappan to Lewis and Charles Tappan, March, 1824.
5. Sarah Tappan to Arthur Tappan, June, 1807.
6. Ibid.
7. Ibid.
8. Tappan, *Op. Cit.,* 41.
9. Ibid., 47.
10. Bertram Wyatt-Brown, *Lewis Tappan and the Evangelical War Against Slavery* (Cleveland, 1969), 4.
11. Tappan, *Op. Cit.,* 17.
12. Diary of Lewis Tappan, May, 1826.

3
Their Spiritual Evolution

NEITHER LEWIS nor Arthur Tappan was greatly involved in the reforming efforts of antebellum America until they were middle-aged. Their involvement, then, was necessarily the result of more than their mother's early firm influence. In order to adequately understand the perspective they themselves had on their reforming endeavors, it would be useful to trace the changes they saw taking place in themselves before their involvement in reform. Very little is known about Arthur's life between his time at home and the point at which he entered the reforming movement. He apparently did not keep a daily journal or even save and file his personal correspondence. What is known of him during these years is found chiefly in Lewis Tappan's biography of his brother. Though the major events of Arthur's life in this period are recorded by Lewis, he does not go into much depth about Arthur's changing ideology, and that which he does say is filtered through his own perspective. But one thing seems certain — Arthur was not really involved in the reform movement until he moved to New York City in the 1820's.

In 1801, nearly fifteen years old, Arthur left his parents to work with his brother John at Sewall and Salisbury, a wholesale importing store in Boston. Arthur had been plagued with daily headaches since childhood, which made long work hours very difficult. He had learned, however, to work and socialize in spite of his pain — an important lesson, as his headaches were to continue throughout his life. His "family" in Boston included not only his brother John, but also his sister Lucy, the wife of the Rev. John Pierce of Brookline, and his uncle, the Rev. Dr. David Tappan, Professor of Divinity at Harvard.

While in Boston, Arthur attended the Federal Street Church where the Rev. William Ellery Channing was the pastor. Channing's eloquence as a preacher was widely acclaimed, and, as Lewis points out in his book, "Mr. Channing was considered at that time an evangelical minister, or something very near it."[1] Although his teaching affected Arthur, it was to play a much greater role in the life of Lewis.

Lewis arrived in Boston in 1804, three years after Arthur, and again at the age of fifteen. He was apprenticed to "a disagreeable man" named Wiggin, who was in the dry goods trade. Although he lived on the third floor of their home, he never really was welcomed into the Wiggin family circle. Instead he spent his free hours with his sister Lucy, the family of his uncle, William Homes (who was operating his father's old goldsmith shop), or sitting wrapped in blankets in his chilly room reading history, trade manuals, or devotional literature. He mastered the double-entry system of bookkeeping, recently imported from abroad, and showed so much inventiveness and promise that he was able to borrow money from Wiggen and his brother John to start his own business in 1809, at the age of twenty.

Lewis first tried his luck with a store in Philadelphia, working with French imports, like his brother John. However, trade was poor due to the Jeffersonian embargo, and he decided to go to England to establish connections with exporters of calicos. Returning, he settled in Eastern Canada. When the war of 1812 with England broke out, he barely managed to escape with his goods before the British confiscated all property owned by American citizens. Prices were rising, and English goods were in high demand in America, and so he made a fortune of $75,000 (equivalent today to $2,250,000).* At this time he was only twenty-three years old.[3]

---

*University of Massachusetts history professor Stephen B. Oates records in his new biography of Lincoln a thirty to one decrease in buying power between 1850 and today.[2] All monetary figures, therefore, for the remainder of the paper, will be followed by the modern equivalent in brackets.

In the meantime, Arthur, who had begun an Indian blanket trading operation in Montreal, lost heavily because of the war. Lewis lent him $12,000 ($360,000) without interest, which Arthur used to start an import firm in New York City. With the rest of his money, Lewis bought a hardware store in Boston. Now financially secure, he married in 1813 Susan Aspinwall, a socially respectable woman seven years his junior.

As Lewis settled into Boston society, he became involved in various benevolent enterprises, including Asylums for the Deaf and Dumb, for the Insane, and for Indigent Boys. He helped start the Boston Provident Institution — the first savings bank in New England — modelled after a British precedent. But one historian notes, Tappan's social concern at this stage was not really demonstrative of a reforming zeal. His aim was not the renovation of society as much as the exercise of a mild benevolence and the improvement of the existing order of things. "Like most of his contemporaries among Boston businessmen, he was a social conservative . . . he considered himself a liberal, generous, and well-informed man who sought only the good of all. His self-satisfaction did not, however, encourage an awareness that something was wrong in the nation that needed instant and wholesale reform; it was a sign of his conformity."[4]

During his time in Boston, Lewis became increasingly devoted to William Ellery Channing — much to the dismay of his mother, who did not consider Channing to be an evangelical. Despite his mother's feelings, Lewis and his family joined Channing's church in 1816. Two years previously, in order to record the texts of sermons he had heard, Lewis had begun his life-long habit of keeping a journal. The contents of the journal later expanded to include his personal thoughts and family records.[5]

Lewis' concern with religious matters was a pronounced factor in his personal writings. On January 1st, 1817 he wrote: "Upon entering a new year it is proper to look back on the past, to see what report it has borne to heaven . . . we have, I hope, made some progress (alas how little!) in the Christian life. God mercifully forgive us our sins, strengthen our good purpose, and enable us to press foreard to the mark, to the prize of the high calling in Christ Jesus."[6] Later on, he laments "how much *resolution* and *perseverance* is necessary to conquer long indulged habits! How much more noble the victory over such than over those more casually to be subdued."[7] Lewis' inability to discipline his actions and feelings to match his religious expectations became a continuing point of frustration during this period of his life.

In the spring of 1817, Lewis Tappan began what was to become a long debate, both within himself, and with others, over the subject of the Trinity. One of the major distinctions between the evangelical and Unitarian persuasions came in the stance taken on the doctrine of the Trinity. The evangelicals believed that God has manifested himself in three manners: as the creator/Father, as the Spirit, and as the 'son'/Redeemer-Messiah Jesus Christ. On the other hand, the Unitarians "acknowledge the divinity but not the deity of the Redeemer."[8] That is to say, Christ was God-like (as we are admonished to strive to become) but he was not God himself. As William Channing preached on April 20, 1820, "The Bible teaches God (not Christ) is to be *worshipped,* still less the Holy Spirit."[9] Lewis writes April 27th, 1817, "I am persuaded that the Trinity is not a scriptural doctrine. I must avow what I believe."[10]

For more than ten years he was to argue this position. Especially persistent adversaries were his mother (until her death) and his sister Eliza. Almost without fail their letters contained some further discussion on the issue. His mother was particularly concerned about Lewis' resultant spiritual state, as he records, "It was a sore affliction to her that any of her children disbelieve the doctrine of the Trinity, which she thought the cornerstone of Christianity, and necessary to salvation. As she thought I was particularly active in diffusing Unitarianism she laboured hard, in conversation and correspondence, to convince me of my error . . ."[11] A few months before her death, in March 1826, she had sent Lewis "a long and solume (sic) letter on the subject of my religious (Unitarian) opinions," to which he answered with an eleven-page letter to demonstrate the sincerity, if not correctness, of his beliefs. Although his mother and sister saw him as distant from God and without a saving knowledge of Him, Lewis viewed himself as quite religious and was at least mildly disturbed by the irreligious and semi-atheistic position taken by his brother Benjamin.

There are other major points of difference between the Unitarian and evangelical/orthodox beliefs that affected the perspectives of Lewis Tappan. First, the Unitarians chose to believe that only parts of the Bible were inspired. Lewis notes in 1820 that:

> W(illiam) C(hanning) thought too that it would be easier to defend the O(ld) T(estament) against scepticks (sic) if we disbelieved the inspiration of certain portions of the O(ld) T(estament). He said it was

not generally believed that the earth was much older than the age of Adam . . . He said Luke and Mark (not being written by apostles) could not be inspired. Matthew also is a translation. Priestly and others think no man was ever inspired except Jesus Christ. The prophets claim inspiration 'Thus saith the Lord' — Moses also — and the apostles. What they have delivered as doctrines or precepts we are to receive as coming from God.[12]

The evangelicals, on the other hand, believed in the inspiration of the Bible in its entirety.

Second, the evangelicals, showing their Calvanist heritage, believed in "original sin"; that is, that since the Fall of Adam, man has had a veil betwen himself and God, created by the separation caused by original sin and greatly heightened by subsequent willful sin on the part of each individual. The Unitarians, on the other hand, believed man to be basically good, with a natural tendency toward living morally, dealing justly, and loving God as neighbor.

Third, the evangelicals saw the "vicarious sacrifice of Christ" as being a necessary prerequisite for the just and complete forgiveness of God which restores communion between men — as individuals accepting his grace — and Himself. The Unitarians or liberals saw such an atonement as unnecessary, Christ being primarily a divinely inspired man who served as an example and teacher for mankind. The Unitarians therefore also rejected the concept of hell — either as an actual physical manifestation or as a metaphoric illustration of the reality of an eternity in complete separation from God (as compared to the partial separation which exists on earth). The "conversion experience" (where one confronts God, turns from his old life, acknowledges the need for forgiveness and the necessary atonement of Christ) was deemed therefore, to be unnecessary by the Unitarians.

The fourth major difference was about a doctrinal point on which even the orthodox were not in agreement. The traditional Calvinists believed in "the election of the saints". This means that God has predestined or "elected" certain people to come to know Him and to live eternally. Beginning with Jonathan Edwards and George Whitefield, this viewpoint was being modified: it was seen as important to seek to "bring all to repentance." Those that did repent and showed a marked change of life were considered to be the "elect", while those that persevered in unbelief ("those who will not believe" as Sarah Tappan said), and died in such a state, were thought obviously not to be among the elect.

Although Lewis decided to reject the doctrinal positions of evangelicalism, he brought with him into his Unitarianism an evangelistic approach to one's own beliefs which was more typical of the evangelicals than of the liberals. From the beginning, he found many of his colleagues, both pastors and laymen, less involved in philanthropy than he would have liked. He worked to raise support for a Unitarian missionary in India. For a while he edited the *Christian Register*, a Unitarian journal, which his brother Charles printed and published. His assistance in institutionalizing the Church is his most permanent contribution: in May, 1825 he catalyzed the formation of the American Unitarian Association and became its first treasurer.[13] Until this time, the Unitarians had been a rather uncertain, amorphous body of Congregationalists. Lewis hoped that organizing would help raise the level of conviction of Unitarians in general; for if their belief was in fact the truth, they should be persuading others of that fact. But despite his efforts, the lack of philanthropic action among Unitarians continued to disappoint him.[14]

Part of Lewis' frustration was perhaps an outward demonstration of his growing frustration with his own life. On May 23rd, 1825 — his 37th birthday — he lamented:

> Old as I am I have not yet acquired that self-government which I have so long made effort to obtain. I am left to make expressions, and to manifest a peevish and irritable humour. Self-government is truly difficult. I have not that devotional spirit I ought to possess. I omit secret prayer or perform it coldly; I do not read alone the sacred scriptures. I do not attend sufficiently to the religious education of my children. O God! So teach me to number my days as to apply my heart unto wisdom. May I remember that the day is far spent that the night cometh in which no man can work.[15]

Later in 1825, Lewis Tappan and his family moved to Brookline where they began attending the church of Rev. Pierce, Lewis' brother-in-law. By this time, the general religious awakening was gaining momentum. By adopting new methods and ideas, the orthodox were creating a general revival in religion, as they worked to counteract the liberal trend of the Unitarian and other movements. This modified-Calvinism, which promoted revivals and voluntary or benevolent associations, came to be known as "evangelicalism." The term was a broad one, cutting across denominational lines. The Congregational denomination split between the Unitarians and orthodox; Rev. Pierce's church also was caught in the conflict. Pierce chose to try to walk a middle ground, avoiding commitment to either the Unitarian or the orthodox factions. The smoldering of submerged controversy, and the frustration with Pierce's unwillingness to commit himself to Unitarianism, caused Lewis to reconsider anew his own beliefs.

In 1826 Lyman Beecher moved to Boston to take the leadership of the interdenominational evangelical faction. He stressed that the essence of Christianity was salvation through the Redeemer rather than the traditional Calvinistic dogma of sovereignty and man's depravity. He also led a pamphlet campaign against the Unitarians, helped organize revivalistic prayer meetings, and encouraged reform. As the Unitarians grew increasingly defensive and critical of the evangelical movement, they withdrew from the benevolent societies, which were dominated by Beecher's Congregational and Presbyterian allies.[16]

Lewis Tappan was stimulated by the increased religious feelings and controversy. He read all the pamphlets, debated the ecclesiastical issue with his friends, and sporadically attended revival services held in his factory shed at Ware, Massachusetts.[17] In early 1827, Lewis and a close friend named William Ropes* introduced monthly prayer meetings to Lewis' town of Brookline. In the process, Lewis became increasingly aware of what he considered to be shortcomings among the Unitarians. Their general lack of interest in foreign missions and domestic revival seemed to him a sign of a lack of Christian spirit. He began noticing "omissions in . . . piety" among those of his denomination; began seeing weaknesses in Unitarian arguments which he had not before noticed. In "the great book of human nature" which he "was daily to read in Brookline" he saw many among the Unitarians to be "deficient in religious character." As he later told his brother Benjamin, ". . . all these things, with others, brot (sic) conviction to my mind that the great body of religious people were of the orthodox denomination, and that the opposite opinions did not produce spirituality of the mind and heart." [19]

The effect one's beliefs had on one's behavior and lifestyle seems to have been an important point in Lewis' mind. He recorded in detail the conversion of his handyman Caleb and remarked on the greater efficiency he showed in his work, and his greater desire to witness to God, in contrast to his previous behavior.[20] After his own

---

*Ropes was a prominent shipper and even carried tracts and Bibles with him on his business trips to Russia.[18]

conversion to orthodoxy/evangelicalism, he tried to persuade his brother-in-law, Rev. Pierce, arguing on the basis of the greater change usually demonstrated in those of that persuasion. He noted changes in conduct, in joyfulness, in repentance, in forgiveness, in love expressed in action, and in witnessing to God's love which he had seen more often occuring from the O(rthodox) preaching."[21]

On October 30th, 1827, Lewis Tappan experienced an encounter with God which quite conclusively settled any remaining doubts he had about the evangelical approach to God. The experience came in the midst of a letter he was writing to his father (his mother had been dead for nearly two years). Later in his journal, he recorded the letter:

> While in the steps I have taken I am not conscious of professing sentiments I have not honestly believed, it has come home to me with power whether I have believed with the heart as well as the head. To this inquiry I am constrained to answer in the negative. And in tracing the effects of religious opinions, and religious instruction, it appears to me that the Unitarian or liberal sentiments do not produce that spirituality of conduct which the gospel enjoins. [At this point in the journal record, Lewis records parenthetically his encounter with God:] When I had written so far I . . . shut the book, and repaired to my library to address my prayer to the Father of Lights. There, on my knees, and with tears, I confessed my errors and my sins, and implored divine illumination. I felt a constraining influence to address God in three persons, and then to pray to Jesus . . . I returned to my desk and finished my letter as follows. [The letter continues:] I shall therefore withdraw myself from the influences of a denomination with which I have cordially and for a long period acted, and shall put myself under the influences of the orthodox denomination, fully aware that such a change, though it may aid me in a pious course, will be ineffectual without the influences I would devoutly supplicate. May I have a father's prayers that the love of God may shed abroad in my heart; that I may be delivered from all worldly biases; that I may humbly seek for light, and openly avow the convictions of my mind; and that with all sincerity and perseverance I may attain to the truth as it is in Jesus. With affectionate regard, your son L.T.[22]

The intellectual reasons for Lewis' conversion are quite often expressed, as he attempted to explain his change of convictions to his many startled and suspicious Unitarian friends. At first he assured them of his sincerity and challenged them to judge his motives by his future conduct.[23] His greatest conflict came with his brother-in-law and pastor Rev. Pierce (whom he had so shortly before tried to persuade to take a firm stand on Unitarianism). Pierce considered Lewis rash and impulsive. Lewis eventually decided to leave Pierce's church in Brookline to get orthodox teaching for himself and his family on a consistent basis. This action greatly disturbed many — at first even his wife strongly objected. Lewis wrote to his sister, Mrs. Pierce, "Of what use is it to keep the people united, if union is to be purchased by suppressing the truth? . . . It grieved us to leave his (Pierce's) m(inistry) and had not we loved our S(aviour) more we could not have done it . . . Let us not cease to love each other . . . It is not a matter of taste, but of conscience with me."[24] Eventually Lewis had to publish a pamphlet setting forth the reasons he claimed as crucial to his decision, in order to counteract rumors. Skirting most theological issues and dismissing the old Calvinist doctrine of election as "a merely speculative subject," he asserted the basic sinfulness of man but emphasized the possibility of redemption through "a careful attention to the means of grace and from special influences of the Holy Spirit."[25]

Perhaps the best summary of Lewis' perspective on his conversion is found in a statement he made to Rev. Pierce, which echoed his mother, though his evangelical theology did not really parallel his mother's at all points. He wrote: "It was a belief in the necessity of a change of heart that was alone or principally to be regarded."[26] Of his own new-found and heartfelt relationship with God, he commented: "What a fool I have been, thought I, to cast from me so much joyful emotion, and to live so long in neglect of sources of so much happiness. O God! may I redeem the time that is past, and work now while the day lasts. It seems as if I had acquired a new sense . . . one of religious sensibility."[27]

NOTES

1. Lewis Tappan, *The Life of Arthur Tappan* (Westport, Conn., 1970), 36.

2. Stephen B. Oates, *With Malice Toward None: The Life of Abraham Lincoln,* as quoted by Arthur P. Bushnell, *Extra,* May 1977, 25.

3. Bertram Wyatt-Brown, *Lewis Tappan and the Evangelical War Against Slavery* (Cleveland, 1969), 18.

4. Ibid., 21-22.

5. Diary of Lewis Tappan, October 22, 1816.

6. Diary, January 1, 1817.

7. Diary, January 11, 1817.

8. Diary, January 25, 1817.

9. Diary, April 20, 1820.

10. Diary, April 27, 1817.

11. Diary, October, 1826.

12. Diary, May 24, 1820.
13. Diary, May 26, 1825.
14. Wyatt-Brown, *Op. Cit.,* 27.
15. Diary, May 23, 1825.
16. Wyatt-Brown, *Op. Cit.,* 29.
17. Diary, November, 1826.
18. Wyatt-Brown, *Op. Cit.,* 30.
19. Diary, November 7, 1827.
20. Wyatt-Brown, *Op. Cit.,* 30.
21. Diary, November 25, 1827.
22. Diary, October 30, 1827.
23. Diary, November 1, 1827.
24. Diary, December 20, 1827.
25. Wyatt-Brown, *Op. Cit.,* 34.
26. Diary, December 8, 1827.
27. Diary, November 3, 1827.

4
English Influence

ALMOST ALL of the evangelical reforming efforts which developed in America were preceded by similar movements in England. Long before American abolitionists got organized, the British agitators were making great headway toward eradicating slavery and the slave trade from the English empire. In fact, with the exception of the American Temperance Society, the American benevolent societies "both in purpose and in method were inspired by British originals."[1] If this evaluation is correct, then the British precedent becomes another important influence on the Tappan brothers. Having already seen the influence which their early upbringing and their later conversion to evangelical Christianity had on their perspectives and motivations, it is important now to look briefly into the nature and source of the British reform movements and the closeness of interaction between them and the Tappans.

Sixty years before the reform movements began in England, the entire country had experienced a powerful awakening led by John Wesley. The Wesleyan "Methodists", as they became called, remained for quite a long time within the established (Anglican) Church of England. They continued to support an authoritarian church discipline and claimed intimate relations with that church. Most of the Methodists were in the rising artisan and trading classes to whom the non-conformist and evangelical spirit of Methodism appealed. Also involved in the movement, however, was a group of evangelicals with the Church of England. "Evangelicalism's most powerful directing force was the group of aristocratic politicians, bankers and Anglican clerics of Clapham and Cambridge who burrowed from within the church establishment."[2] Frequently gathering in the home of one of the leaders, William Wilberforce, in Clapham (then a suburb of London), the group of evangelical philanthropists became known as the "Clapham Sect." Not a formal religious party, and all members of the Church of England, they were frequently denounced by High Anglican Tories as Methodists. As one historian puts it: "Though connected with what we have called 'the establishment', evangelicalism was essentially rebellious and disruptive, and brought considerable strength to the mobilized forces of Dissent. For, in the words of an Anglican historian, the evangelicals 'cared little for the Church or for the State as a Divine institution. Their business was with personal salvation, with individuals as opposed to corporate religion.' Thus they encouraged a non-denominational temper, represented by the Evangelical Alliance of 1846 which united Anglicans and Non-conformists, and they were prepared to work with all Churches on both sides of the Atlantic in moral reform."[3]

The Evangelical Awakening in both England and America may be said to have originated mainly in the ministries of the two Englishmen John Wesley and George Whitefield. America's great leader during this era of revival was Jonathan Edwards, and it was the same united Evangelical Awakening that had led to the conversion of Sarah Tappan. The transatlantic connection was strong, and was to remain so throughout the resultant reforming era. William Wilberforce's *Practical View* ran through an edition each year in the United States from 1800 to 1826.[4] In turn, Whitefield's revival tours through American back country from Georgia to Massachusetts eventually resulted in a backwoods influence on the revivalism techniques of evangelists in England — with camp meetings imported from Western New York and the urban crusade imported from the examples set by Finney and the Tappans in New York City. Wesley himself had instituted very substantial extension training (due to the shortage of trained clergy) and had started the practice of circuit riding and open-air preaching which was long to be foundational to the Western American churches. In 1844 Charles Finney, on an evangelistic tour in England, inspired George Williams, a young London shop assistant, to start the Young Men's Christian Association.[5] The Y.M.C.A. soon found its way to America where it was influential in getting young men into Bible studies and organized outreach. The interaction was great, each country affecting the other "in the common object of spiritual regeneration and moral reform. 'Unite Britain and America in energetic and resolved co-operation for the world's salvation,' wrote two Congregationalist delegates from Britain to the United States in 1836, 'and the world is saved.' They spoke for a generation of earnest souls whose brisk traffic across the Atlantic was concerned with nothing less than world salvation."[6]

With a greater perspective on the world horizons, the British evangelicals took the initiative in missionary activities and moral reform movements. Wilberforce's first preoccupation, the Society for the Suppression of Vice, led to the formation of a society by the same name in New York in 1802. Englishman Robert Raike's Sunday School (1788) was followed by the Philadelphia First Day Society of 1790 and later the American Sunday School Union. "Independently, Samuel Slater had carried in his head to Rhode Island the model not merely of his erstwhile employer's spinning frame, but of his Belper Sunday School."[7] Hannah More's Religious Tract Society (1799) was later copied in New England (1814) to be followed in 1823 by the American Tract Society. The great British overseas missionary societies, including William Carey's Baptist Missionary Society, the non-denominational London Missionary Society (1795) and the (Anglican) Church Missionary Society were reflected in the American Home Missionary Society and the American Board of Commissioners for Foreign Missions, while William Carey's letters home from India were being read on both sides of the Atlantic. The British concern for the lack of Bibles, especially among the Welsh and Canadian Indians, led in 1804 to the founding of the British and Foreign Bible Society. The Philadelphia Bible Society (1808) and hundreds of other local societies were followed by the American Bible Society in 1816. Similarly, the London Peace Society (1816) led to the formation of the American Peace Society (1828).

There was one well-known organized reform movement which was initiated in America and went to England: the temperance movement. Even here Wesley had been outspoken against the use of "spiritous liquor," seeing what damage it had done to the families of his recently converted Welsh and Cornwall miners. But the movement as a movement went hand in hand with the American evangelical revival under the ministries of Charles Finney and especially Theodore Weld. It was in America that the temperance movement had developed state societies, city societies, and township societies. "New York State Society, the largest federation, boasted two thousand locals [local societies] in 1833, with young men's societies, infant societies, and female auxiliaries; and during that year it printed eighty-nine million pages of propaganda."[8] At almost the same time, efforts among evangelicals in England to combat drunkenness became manifest. However, its origins and chief leadership were American. The American Society for the Promotion of Temperance was organized in 1826, followed by the British and Foreign Temperance Society in England (1831). Within a year, the British society had fifty-five auxiliary societies, and had published nearly one hundred thousand pamphlets.[9] Both societies were soon split as radicals within them pushed for total abstinence — the term "teetotal" was probably coined in England. Two new societies resulted from the split, based on the tenent of total abstinence: the American Temperance Union (1833) and the British and Foreign Society for the Suppression of Intemperance (1837); the youth contingent was active in the form of "Bands of Hope" in England and "Cold Water Armies" in America. The two movements, American and British, jointly ran the World Temperance Convention in London in 1846.

The Tappans, aware of many of the English reforming endeavors since childhood, watched England closely, especially after their conversions awakened in them a growing interest in the reform of America. Trips across the Atlantic were not infrequent for many of the reformers and revivalists. Lewis sometimes combined business with reforming interests, attending quite a number of London-based world conventions for various reforms. Arthur corresponded personally with William Wilberforce in order to discuss the procedings and methods of various reforming endeavors.

Thus, the high motivation encouraged by their upbringing and established in their conversion experiences was directed and stimulated in interaction with leaders of reform of both England and America. The two countries were, in effect, outdoing each other with good works — a Biblical injunction. Ideas and techniques flowed across the seas in both directions; encouraged by the reforms going on around them, the Tappan brothers began channeling their own resources and energy into reform: of their business, their society, their world.

NOTES

1. Gilbert H. Barnes, *The Anti-Slavery Impulse 1830-1844* (New York, 1933), 18.
2. Frank Thistlethwaite, "The Anglo-American World" in David Brion Davis, ed., *Ante-Bellum Reform* (New York, 1967), 68.
3. Loc. Cit.
4. Ibid., 69.
5. Ibid., 70.
6. Ibid., 71.
7. Loc. Cit.
8. Barnes, *Op. Cit.*, 18.
9. Thistlethwaite, *Op. Cit.*, 76.

5
Reforming—
The Tappans' Business

BECAUSE OF increasing financial difficulties, Lewis Tappan moved to New York in February of 1828 to join his brother Arthur in his now-prosperous silk-importing business. Until this time, apparently neither Lewis nor Arthur had been greatly involved in reform. However, Arthur had for several years been involved in evangelical spheres (which Lewis was now ready to join) and had begun a work of philanthropic giving. As one historian notes, "At first they merely supported various societies very generously. But after (Charles G.) Finney came to N.Y. they took a more active part." Instead of just displaying a benevolent attitude, they began to actually participate to the extent that they were willing to risk their finances and reputations. One of the first areas in which they began to make costly risks and commitments was in the area of business.

The evangelical assertion was that "benevolence was an infinite concern for other people's souls . . . the test of an individual's conversion from sin was his secular action."[2] The Tappans expressed their conversions first, then, by setting their own

"house" in order. In the management of his business, Arthur
Tappan sought to follow Biblical instruction, even when contrary to
the current practices.

He sold for cash or quickly redeemable promissory notes, at fixed
prices, and avoided long-term loans and the usurious rates
associated with them. "He made his profits from, in a phrase, low
markup and high volume. Such innovations evoked wonder, since
the stores on London's Regent Street allowed Arabian haggling over
prices."[3]

Arthur also chose to hold a strict paternal influence over those
young men who were apprenticed into his care. He expected them
to attend church at least once a week; theatres or actresses were
off-limits. In the house that functioned as a dormitory, there was a
room set aside on the third floor known as the "Bethel." It was to be
used for the reading of morning prayers, the performance of
devotionals, and for personal meditation and repentance, especially
during revival seasons. The pay was not very good, and his rules
were harsh, but Arthur was generous in helping the promising
graduates start their own independent careers, which made the
rigorous course worth the trouble.[4]

Lewis and Arthur sought to affect the treatment of apprentices by
other businessmen as well. In 1828 the *New York Evangelist* noted a
speech by Lewis Tappan: "Mr. T(appan) concluded by an appeal to
the merchants to extend a generous, friendly, and paternal care
towards their clerks. To allow them a respectable support — time for
improvement; — to advance their welfare as they approached
manhood — to assist the meritorious, as they become of age — to
extend a liberal aid and fostering care . . . He conjured them to
remember their own feelings at that age and to follow the Golden
Rule, by doing for the young and deserving, what they would have
wished been done for them when commencing their mercantile
career."[5]

Arthur set a strict example for others. " 'A cracker and a tumbler
of cold water sufficed for Arthur's luncheon', Lewis later recalled.
Arthur's family expenses were equally modest, because money, he
believed, was entrusted by God to his care."[6] This basic attitude
toward possessions eventually led Arthur and Lewis Tappan to
organize and found the Association of Gentlemen. As the *New York
Evangelist* (a Christian newspaper founded by the Tappans) records
in 1834: "believing that the accumulation of property for selfish
purposes is repugnant to the gospel; that every person is a steward,
(the Tappans and their associates in philanthropy entered) into a

solemn engagement not to lay up any property we may hereafter acquire . . . but to consecrate the whole of it to the Lord, dedicating sufficient to supply ourselves and families, in a decent manner, as becomes those professing Godliness."[7] The Association of Gentlemen, founded in 1828, was a sort of religious club whose membership consisted of over a dozen wealthy men, mostly from rural Connecticut and in the mercantile and banking trades. The association was to take up many benevolent campaigns, one of the more difficult being a revival in New York City which would bring about both the rededication of old church members and the addition of new. To push their campaign forward, the Association of Gentlemen chose two tools: a journal to publicize revivals and benevolent enterprises (the *New York Evangelist)* and a revival in the churches of the city to be led by Charles Grandison Finney. However, when the Tappans took up the anti-slavery cause, their associates were not so quick to become involved. This discrepancy of interest and lack of a cohesive mutual trust, eventually led to the dissolution of the Association.

In the process of bringing their business lives under a reformer's scrutiny, the Tappans started other organizations as well, not the least of which were the Mercantile Library Association and the Mercantile Agency. The Library Association was set up primarily to insure the availability of good books "in every department of literature and science,"[8] for the young apprentices in the city to read and keep them from the temptations of city life. The Mercantile Agency was a credit-rating organization which is better known by its later name of Dun and Bradstreet. Before the Panic of 1837, Arthur Tappan had allowed a continuingly larger number of people to buy from him on credit. As a result, his own company was pulled into bankruptcy in 1837. Having to borrow some money himself to get back on his feet, he managed to pay off all of his former debts, but he also resolved always to allow people to buy on credit, as he was so grateful for the leniency shown to him. Lewis, however, was not at all in agreement with Arthur's decisions.[9] Because of his experiences in Arthur's company during the Panic of 1837, he saw the great need for records of peoples' credit evaluations.

Lewis was adamantly against the greed and material ambitions which he thought the credit system encouraged. In 1869 he wrote a pamphlet called "Is It Right to Be Rich?" in which he stated: ". . . eagerness to amass property . . . robs a man and his family of rational enjoyment . . . (and) . . . tempts him to doubtful and disreputable acts." In 1843 he had written to his brother Benjamin,

"How much wisdom there is in the advice of the apostle Paul — 'owe no man anything — but to love one another'."[10]

It may seem ironic, then, that he founded a company which depended on other people's need (and greed) for credit. Realizing that borrowing could not be abolished in the near future, he reasoned instead that he would seek to make it a more honest and reliable transaction than it had been. He also realized that such an organization would be free, to some extent, from the vicissitudes of the economy. In writing to a nephew he pointed out, "In prosperous times they will feel able to pay for the information and in bad times they feel they must have it."[11]

Lewis found it quite difficult, however, to start his credit rating agency. He needed honest informants in every part of the country in order to insure accurate reports on the people desiring credit. His anti-slavery reputation, however, made few Southerners willing to cooperate, and many New York businesses refused to do business with him for the same reason. He made things even harder for himself by refusing to do business with distilleries, due to his temperance beliefs. What kept him determined to succeed in this was, to a great extent, his belief that God wanted him to do it: "while I wondered that the Lord should have directed my mind to this new employment, and then disappointed me in my expectations, I was brought into sweet submission to His will."[12]

In spite of difficulties, Lewis found his venture to be financially profitable. The first few years had to be spent in adjusting to the many new problems encountered in establishing such an entirely unprecedented type of operation. However, within a year of the founding of the Mercantile Agency other large-scale credit operations were springing up in competition, most without the stigma attached to Lewis' company because of his adamant reforming efforts, especially in the area of slavery. Even in the face of severe opposition on the part of a partner, Edward Dunbar, Lewis chose to continue his reform work. Dunbar resented the time Lewis spent in anti-slavery affairs, feeling they were detrimental to the business. He also felt Lewis' efforts were hypocritical and avaricious rather than pious and philanthropic.[13] However, to Lewis moral issues were of primary importance. His financial welfare and even his reputation with others was of less value to him. This attitude he expressed to Dunbar, saying: "My reputation is a thing upon which I place no value, and I shall never do anything to bolster it up or compensate for its loss."[14]

NOTES

1. Gilbert H. Barnes, *The Anti-Slavery Impulse 1830-1833* (New York, 1933), 20.

2. Clifford S. Griffen, "Religious Benevolence as Social Control, 1815-1816" in David Brion Davis, ed., *Ante-Bellum Reform* (New York, 1967), 85.

3. Bertram Wyatt-Brown, *Lewis Tappan and the Evangelical War Against Slavery* (Cleveland, 1969), 44.

4. Loc. Cit.

5. New York *Evangelist*, May 22, 1828.

6. Wyatt-Brown, *Op. Cit.*, 45.

7. New York *Evangelist*, Vol. II, 71.

8. Ibid., November 2, 1829.

9. Wyatt-Brown, *Op. Cit.*, 227.

10. Lewis Tappan to Benjamin Tappan, December 12, 1843.

11. Quoted from Wyatt-Brown, *Op. Cit.*, 229.

12. Diary, August 10, 1841.

13. Wyatt-Brown, *Op. Cit.*, 239.

14. Lewis Tappan to Edward Dunbar, January 5, 1846.

6

The Evangelical Mandate

MANY OF the Tappan's specific attitudes toward reform and reforming interests were, in part, products of their own lively enthusiasm and particular perspective. But the overall scope of their attitudes were framed and shaped by the radical mindset of the reforming evangelicals. The Tappans' constant interaction with such influential evangelical leaders as Charles Finney, Lyman Beecher, and Theodore Weld produced a great impact on the direction and priorities of their reforms, even though, at points, they had major disagreements with each one. The emphases of these leaders and the Tappans' reactions to them, form an important background for a closer understanding of the standards the Tappans used in shaping their own activities and motives.

By the time the Tappans joined the cause, in the late 1820's, the evangelical revival was already far-reaching in its influence, having affected up to 25% of the American population. While Charles Finney is the best-remembered leader of the West, Lyman Beecher, father of Harriet Beecher Stowe, is probably the best-remembered of the Eastern clergy leaders. The revival caused widespread changes in the Protestant churches that were involved. One historian enumerated what he feels to be four fundamental changes: 1) less clergy control, much more lay participation and control in churches; 2) a spirit of interdenominational brotherhood; 3) ethical concerns rather than dogmatic zeal in evangelical preaching and writing; 4) a modified Calvinism replacing extreme Calvinism.[1] Another important change was a more liberal attitude toward the public role of women. A noted example was the Grimke sisters, Angelina and Sarah, who gave anti-slavery lectures to mixed audiences. Angelina later married Theodore Weld, who is thought, by many historians, to be the most influential of the antebellum evangelical abolitionists.

The increased level of lay participation was both a natural and necessary result of the theology of the transformed life preached by the revivalists. "Finney made salvation the beginning of religious experience instead of its end. The emotional impulse which Calvinism had concentrated upon a painful quest for a safe escape from life, Finney thus turned toward benevolent activity."[2] Finney believed that men and women were converted not so much for their own salvation, but so that they could begin a new life "in the interests of God's kingdom." In this new life, Finney stated "They have no separate interests . . . they should set out with a determination to *aim at being useful in the highest degree possible.*"[3] As late as 1868, Charles Finney continued to insist that "the loss of interest in benevolent enterprises" was usually evidence of a "backslidden heart." Among these enterprises Finney specified "good government, Christian education, temperance reform, the abolition of slavery, and relief for the poor."[4]

The spirit of interdenominational brotherhood both rose and waned with the revival, which was strongest between 1815 and 1835. Presbyterians and Congregationalists, joined by a smaller number of Methodists, Baptists and Episcopalians, composed the core of the revival or evangelical movement. The Tappans, for example, referred to themselves as orthodox or evangelical although for the greater part of their reforming careers they could most likely be associated primarily with the "New School" Presbyterians (contrasted with the more traditionally Calvinist "Old School" Presbyterians, a group almost equal in size and not in favor of revivalism). These five denominations, seeking to supply the religious needs of the expanding country, formed five great national interdenominational societies between 1815 and 1829: The American Education Society, American Home Missionary Society,

American Bible Society, American Tract Society, and the American Sunday School Union. These societies were seen primarily as a means of more effectively reaching sinners.

> The societies stressed Christ's atonement, the mercy God offered and the grace which God would grant to those who repented and believed . . . As interpreted by the societies, benevolence — or, as it was often called, charity, or love for man — was the idea that certain persons, having received God's sanctified grace, were obliged to extend to all men, the means of obtaining that grace . . . God's mercy was the greatest gift anyone could receive; love, which was the fulfilling of the Law, directed and sanctified to share this gift.[5]

Both the emphases of Finney and the central concerns of the interdenominational societies show the interweaving of ethical concerns with evangelism (seen as a benevolent sharing of grace rather than a dogmatic debate over theological issues). The prevailing attitude toward theology among evangelicals was expressed well by Lewis Tappan himself as he urged Theodore Weld to come to New York City to evangelize: " 'A powerful inroad may be made here . . . into the dominions of Satan . . . As to your not having studied Theology . . . there is too much Theology in the church now, and too little of the gospel!' "[6] The stress on ethical issues and a changed lifestyle, and the preaching of the gospel were the two central foci of the evangelical revival. Rarely did evangelicals distinguish between the two.

In their personal lives, Lewis and Arthur demonstrated the same dual emphases. Lewis can be especially noted for his personal commitment to the evangelizing of others. In company with Rev. Joshua Leavitt, a young minister from Yale Seminary who later served as the editor of the New York *Evangelist,* Lewis Tappan would spend hours passing out Bibles and Tracts. They roamed the wharves of the East River; they entered the dingy stores and taverns of Five Points (one of the worst districts of New York City); and they stopped in the counting houses of Wall and State Streets. To each person they gave a tract. By May 1831, Lewis Tappan and others had distributed over six million pages.[7] One Sunday Lewis recorded in his journal that he had visited 40 vessels, distributing tracts and talking with the seamen. Tracts were not always received well — he noted that they were rebuffed a couple of times — but he seemed happy that in most cases "the tracts were re(ceive)d thankfully."[8]

Lewis' involvement in personal evangelism was also directed toward his family, as his mother's had been. Family devotions were held nightly and his journal contains periodic records of the welfare and spiritual state of his children along with prayers for their spiritual and physical health. He persevered in his attempt to convert his deistic brother, Benjamin. He charged his brother to analyze the "effects of religion" on people's lives in comparison to the effects of living without it. Becoming more specific: "I allude not to particular cases, but to mankind in general; nor do I allude to all that goes by the name of religion, but to Christianity as believed and practised by the gr(ea)t body of Christian people."[9] He allowed for the possibility that Benjamin could come up with an answer opposing Christianity, and, unlike his mother, admitted his inability to persuade further, if such should happen. However, Lewis did make one request, which shows the respect he had for the power of the Bible: "You will permit me, my brother, affectionately to ask you to read the New Testament in a candid state of mind, as if you had never read anything opposed to it, and read it as a book wh(ich) *may* be true, and wh(ich) very many think is true. I pray God to guide you in this course."[10] When Benjamin was elected to the United States Senate, Lewis wrote: "To tell you the honest truth I should have preferred to have heard that you had become a sincere deacon of a church."[11] The primary necessity and importance of a sincere conversion and personal knowledge of God was foremost in Lewis' mind — and he saw it as his personal responsibility to share his experience with others.

Lewis' concern to reach others with the gospel was demonstrated in other ways as well. Early in 1828, he and his brother Arthur caught a vision for what they termed "colonizing churches." Apparently this involved persuading some of the existing large evangelical congregations to send out a nucleus of committed people to start new churches in other parts of the city where they thought there was no effective Christian outreach.

New York   16 Feb. 1828

Rev. Dr. Beecher. As I shall have some leisure here it is my wish to devote it to some useful purpose, and religious operations will be more congenial with my feelings than any other. From some observations already made I am led to believe that the evangelical churches in this city have no unity of action for the general cause of Christianity; that many of them are overgrown, and of course keep in obscurity many persons who might be highly useful; that the principal clergy are timid or indecisive; that considerable numbers of laymen are in advance of their "spiritual guides" respecting the best means of extending religion; that many professors — the N.E. men in particular — are not partial to Presbyterianism; that there are enough

Sons of Pilgrims in this city to subscribe $30,000 in shares of $100 for
the purpose of building a new church."[12]

He goes on to propose specific steps to be taken toward the
establishment of the "First Colonization Church in the City of N.Y.

The idea seemed obvious to them. The large churches were
bursting with leadership which was not fully used. Further, if those
Christians really wanted to win others to Christ, would they not
happily go where they were needed, and wouldn't their pastors
send them on their way with their blessings? But, persuading
church leaders of this plan was not as simple as they had originally
anticipated. Lewis recorded his frustration in his journal: "Those
who profess to feel the importance of colonizing churches shrink, at
our meetings, from taking the decided stand the times require . . . O
God! awaken this people; arouse the ministers and their people."[13]

Because the churches did not respond to their persuasions, the
two brothers turned instead to founding churches themselves. The
most famous was the Chatham Street Chapel, which met in a large
theatre that they rented and converted to a church. It was dedicated
on April 23, 1832,[14] with the financial backing of the Association of
Gentlemen. The church, located near the Five Points slum district,
had two distinctions: First, it was one of the first "free churches"
where no pew rentals were charged, but voluntary offerings were
collected. This enabled the poor and rich to sit intermingled, as
Lewis preferred. Second, the Tappans — with great difficulty —
persuaded Charles Finney to leave his western revival efforts to
come lead a revival in this church in New York City. Lewis wrote to
Finney. "I do not think a powerful revival will take place here unless
you do come . . . Do what may be done elsewhere, and leave this
city the headquarters of Satan, and the nation is not saved . . . A
blow struck here reverberates to the extremities of the republic."[15]

Although both evangelism and the moral reform of society were
each central concerns to the reformers like the Tappans and to the
evangelists like Charles Finney, the priorities they placed on each
were different. With the same goal (the evangelization of the world)
and the same Christian values, the reformers and the evangelists
nevertheless approached from opposite directions the task of
changing mankind. Finney continually emphasized the need for
persuasive evangelism first, converting nominal Christians and
non-Christians to a sincere and deep relationship with God. Reform
of one's lifestyle, he contended, must follow. The Tappans, on the
other hand, could not see how anyone could be converted until the

existing Christians had purified their own lifestyle. Therefore, reform had to come first; evangelism would then naturally follow. Lewis showed his progression of thinking when he recorded in his journal (after attending a meeting of the Committee on the Observance of the Sabbath, April 19, 1828): "Professors of r(religion) declaim much ag(ains)t the infidelity and wickednees of the world, but if they understood and did their master's will, shining as lights in the world, with a steady lustre, the world would be evangelized."[16]

The importance of reform in the Tappans' minds extended beyond merely the great effect a good example would have on the evangelization of the world. The lack of a Christ-like lifestyle among Christians, especially clergy, was, in their minds, actually hindering the cause of Christ in America and the world. "I consider that the ministers of the gospel, at the present," Lewis wrote to his cousin Eliza Bigelow in 1843, "are doing more to disaffect the ungodly against religion and to grieve the Holy Spirit, by their deviant opposition to the righteous claims of humanity than all the infidels in the country. There are a few noble exceptions."[17]

Over a period of time the Tappans increased their emphasis on reform issues, and consequently began to experience a break with their friend Charles Finney. Beginning at Chatham Street Chapel, and later at Oberlin College, Finney exerted his authority to insure that a person's personal confrontation with God would not be displaced in importance by the issues of moral reform. Although himself an adamant abolitionist and teetotaler, he maintained his conviction that the foundational issue, and therefore central concern, was a person's response to God. Training his students to be evangelists, he refused to follow the Tappan's exhortations to make them into abolitionist preachers. However, in spite of their different approaches, they both held as their goal the evangelization of the world. This fact served as a bridge of friendship between them and also, in a certain sense, between the many evangelicals with all their varying perspectives on how to achieve that goal.

NOTES

1. Timothy L. Smith, *Revivalism and Social Reform: American Protestantism on the Eve of the Civil War* (New York, 1965 ed.), 80.
2. Gilbert H. Barnes, *The Anti-Slavery Impulse 1830-1844* (New York, 1933), 11.
3. Charles Grandison Finney, *Revival Lectures* (New York), 374-5.
4. Smith, *Op. Cit.*, 60.
5. Clifford S. Griffen, "Religious Benevolence as Social Control, 1815-1816" in David Brion Davis, ed., *Ante-Bellum Reform* (New York, 1967), 83.

6. Quoted from Gilbert H. Barnes, *The Anti-Slavery Impulse 1830-1844* (New York, 1933), 15.

7. Bertram Wyatt-Brown, *Lewis Tappan and the Evangelical War Against Slavery* (Cleveland, 1969), 53.

8. Diary, March 16, 1828.

9. Lewis Tappan to Benjamin Tappan, March 14, 1828.

10. Loc. Cit.

11. Quoted from Benjamin P. Thomas, *Theodore Weld: Crusader for Freedom* (New Brunswick, 1950), 30.

12. Lewis Tappan to Lyman Beecher, February 16, 1828.

13. Diary, March 7, 1828.

14. Bernard A. Weisberger, *They Gathered at the River: The Story of Revivalists and Their Impact Upon Religion in America* (Boston, 1958), 126.

15. Quoted from Weisberger, *Op. Cit.,* 124-125.

16. Diary, April 19, 1928.

17. Lewis Tappan to Eliza Bigelow, December 26, 1843.

7

Overhauling Society

NOT CONTENT with the state of affairs in the United States, the Tappans set out to reform first their own New York City, and subsequently the world. Their activities, interests, and benevolent concerns were numerous — to merely list them would take several pages. Of the two brothers, Arthur was the more prominent in reforming circles. This was not, however, because he was abler or more philanthropic, but because Lewis often chose to relieve him of the tedium of business affairs in order that he could spend more time doing good works. But, as one historian points out, Lewis was "in some respects more zealous in reform; he was also more impetuous and tenacious. When Arthur became discouraged, Lewis took over. But impetuosity sometimes forced him to reconsider, so he was thought to vacillate."[1] Though their approaches differed somewhat, their concerns were nearly completely the same. Vary rarely was one involved in a cause without the other; equally rarely were they in disagreement about the stance to take on a certain issue.

The Tappans' involvement in reform covered a wide spectrum of causes. To attempt to analyze their efforts chronologically would be confusing, at best. Therefore, as each of their major reforming efforts is discussed, or merely noted, it must be kept in mind that their involvement was simultaneous. Otherwise, one could get the impression that they were extremely inconsistent in their concerns, rather than universal and comprehensive.

By the time the Tappans began to get actively involved in evangelical reforming circles, many societies were already strong and widespread, most notably the five great interdenominational societies founded between 1815 and 1820. The brothers had begun their benevolent careers by contributing generously to these five societies and also to earlier societies such as the American Board of Commissioners for Foreign Missions, founded in 1810 by Lyman Beecher and others. Since his Unitarian days, Lewis had already been giving some support to the American Bible Society.

Soon after his conversion, Lewis joined the growing movement of evangelicals working to bring about a more conscientious observance of the Sabbath. He became the corresponding secretary of a society to prevent the Sunday conveyance of mail, fighting the congressional act requiring postal clerks to work on Sunday.[2] Joining the General Union for Promoting the Observance of the Christian Sabbath, he also worked against the use of illuminating gas in churches in order that gas workers might be free to worship on the Lord's Day.[3] "If it be necessary," Lewis wrote in the New York *Evangelist*, "to violate the holy Sabbath habitually in order to manufacture any article of luxury or convenience, Christians ought to dispense with the use of such articles."[4] As secretary of the Sabbath Union, he backed a six-day stage coach called the Pioneer. Good Christians were expected to travel on this stage rather than on those that moved on Sunday. This cause proved a financial disaster, and Lewis and the other "Sabbatarians" were ridiculed, in particular by the Universalists, for their efforts to promote perfect Sabbath-keeping. Lewis was nettled with sarcastic accusations that the silk he sold was "un-Christian" since the worms worked on the Sabbath; his discouragement was heightened by Congress' continued refusal to repeal the offending postal statutes. It was not until Lewis had essentially gone on to other causes that Sabbatarianism gathered enough strength, in 1843, to induce the sympathetic Charles Sickliffe, Postmaster General in John Tyler's cabinet, to close down 80,000 miles of postal routes on the Lord's day.[5]

In 1827, Arthur founded the New York *Journal of Commerce*, with the aim of bringing a wholesome moral influence to the newspaper field. His paper accepted no "immoral" advertisements, such as those for theaters, circuses, or spiritous liquors. No issue appeared on Sunday, and Monday's issue was ready for distribution by 12 o'clock Saturday night so that no work would be done on Sunday.[6] His newspaper was innovative not only on a moral level, but on other levels as well. For example, he infuriated the existing newspapers when he acquired a small boat to meet the incoming vessels from other parts of the world, thereby getting their news several hours in advance. Distributed free of charge at first, the paper soon caused Arthur to lose 30,000 dollars. He then turned it over to Lewis. As the previous editor, Rev. William Maxwell, had been unable to prove that religious and commercial news could profitably flourish in the same journal, Lewis changed editors. Nevertheless, he was still forced to sell the paper to a Connecticut evangelical named David Hale, under whose direction it quickly grew into a leading financial and political sheet and continues in publication to this day.[7]

Among the Tappan's benefactions were a number of educational institutions, including Auburn Theological Seminary, Kenyon College and the Oneida Institute. At one time or another, they gave financial aid to more than one hundred divinity students at Yale.[8] But their interest in the actual process of education was not great until their own sons were involved in it. After noticing, with apprehension, the growing atheism of his oldest son, William, Lewis decided on the advice of Charles Finney to send him and his younger son to the Oneida Institute at Whitesboro, New York. This step was significant for two reasons. First, Oneida was one of the first American schools to adopt the system of manual labor-education. Second, Theodore Weld, though in his mid-twenties and already famous as a temperance orator, was in attendance there.

The system of manual labor-education required that each student pay part of his expenses by doing some sort of manual labor on the school farm. Its supposed benefits — improvement of student health and reduction of the cost of education — were especially needed in theological seminaries. Following Oneida's lead, many schools adopted the idea. At Andover Theological Seminary, the trustees built a workshop which would employ seventy-five students. Maine Wesleyan Seminary had both a shop and a farm of 140 acres. However, while at most institutions manual labor was optional, at Oneida it was compulsory.[9]

Lewis Tappan was soon enamoured with the system. He wrote with evident pride to his brother, "My sons are at a school where all the students work on a farm three hours every day . . . It has been the disgrace of this country that education has made most men ashamed of manual labor."[10] Although the idea was already quite popular (by the time Weld enrolled at Oneida, it had sixty students — its capacity — and some six hundred applicants were being turned away)[11] Lewis set out to insure that this excellent idea would be effectively spread. In July, 1831, the Tappan brothers organized a Society for Promoting Manual Labor in Literary Institutions. Lewis Tappan had met Theodore Weld on one of his visits to Oneida and recognized his great leadership potential. Bringing him to New York, the Tappans first attempted to persuade him to accept the pastorate of another "free church" which was to be established as a result of the popularity of the free church they had founded for Finney in the Chatham Street Theatre. When Weld refused, insisting he was not ready for the ministry, they offered him the job of heading up the manual labor education movement instead. At this point in time "manual labor was second only to temperance in Weld's esteem"[12] and, after preaching a series of successful temperance lectures in New York, he decided to accept the job — on the condition that he could do temperance lectures on the side. In his subsequent year-long lecture tour covering 4,575 miles (1800 on horseback), he lectured on temperance, manual labor, and occasionally female education.[13]

The Tappans' interest in education was not limited to manual labor reform. Their original interest was, and continued to be, Christian education as a means of evangelism and discipleship. In the mid-1820's, Arthur had offered the American Sunday School Union $4,000 ($120,000), conditional upon the raising of $100,000 ($3,000,000) from other sources, for the purpose of filling the religious needs of the Mississippi Valley settlers. His desire was that the Union establish a Sunday School in every town in the Mississippi Valley within two years. On the frontier and in port cities and industrial towns the Sunday Schools often furnished the only education of any sort for the poor boys. Slater, who had founded the first weaving industry in America, founded almost simultaneously a Sunday School to teach the factory boys to read and do simple arithmetic. Arthur was interested in this aspect of Sunday Schools also, and logically became in 1826 the president of the reorganized American Education Society. He also was involved in the encouragement of support of theological institutions and pre-ministerial undergraduates, his interest again centering to some extent on the Western areas, mainly through the influence of the American Home Missionary Society which felt that the future of the nation depended on the care given to these growing Western areas.

Perhaps in part due to the influence of Theodore Weld and Charles Finney, the Tappans became increasingly interested in temperance. In 1826 the American Society for the Promotion of Temperance had been formed to advocate drinking in moderation and the avoiding of strong alcoholic beverages. Although many of the earliest temperance advocates were adverse to taking a stand against beer or wine, the evangelicals began to push for a pledge of total abstinence. By 1833 the controversy had caused such a split that the American Temperance Union was founded on the basis of total abstinence. As the movement gained momentum with the preaching of Theodore Weld and others, temperance hotels (where no alcohol was served) were established in New England. Concern for temperance among youth promoted Cold Water Armies in America and Bands of Hope in England. Concern for the cure of the drunkard (in addition to prevention of drunkenness) became widespread.

As Lewis correctly boasted, there was nothing "half-way" about the Tappan brothers' interests and measures.[15] This characteristic can be seen especially clearly in their temperance efforts. Being in favor of total abstinence, they found themselves facing a formidable adversary. While wines and beers were the standard drinking beverage, they also had to contend with the low prices of rum and whiskey. Persuasion not being sufficient, the Tappans resorted to coercive measures. They organized Christian spy cells to watch tavern-keepers and other "dispensers of pleasure" and report the infractions of long-ignored city ordinances to the proper authorities.[16] Arthur set up a fund of $2,000 for those congregations in the Home Missionary "diocese" that expelled drinkers from their churches.

With their use of warning posters plastered on the walls of Manhattan, and tracts and papers declaring the physically disastrous effects of prolonged indulgence in alcoholic beverages, the Tappans were quick to arouse widespread opposition, including some from evangelicals such as Lyman Beecher, who objected to their methods. One poem poked fun at a total abstinence which did not include communion wine in its targets:

> Arthur Tappan, Arthur Tappan
> Suppose it should happen—

> Mind, I'm only *supposing* it should—
> That some folks in the Union
> Should take your *communion*
> Too often by far for their good. [17]

So, the Tappans came up with their own solution to the nation's drinking problem — a substitute beverage, hopefully palatable enough to "entice the intemperate away from vice."[18] Arthur arranged to import a "non-alcoholic" burgundy from France. This "pure juice of the grape" (also referred to as "pure wine" — free from all poisonous substances), was intended to replace communion wine. He also advertized it and added it to his list of goods at his store.[19]

Although some churches availed themselves of the opportunity to eliminate something which had become controversial, many were unsure that to take such a course would be faithful to the Biblical example of communion. Arthur Tappan believed that alcoholic wines were not used by the early Christians. "But whether used by them or not, he held that Christians at the present day are bound to abstain from their use," Lewis recalls, "if detrimental to others."[20] Lewis went on to point out that at least wine was not used in *communion* in the early church for the passover of that period did not use alcoholic wine: "A distinguished Jew in New York, during the controversy, stated in his daily paper that *unfermented* wine was used at the Passover by the Israelites. The editor, Mordecai Manasseh Noah, was deemed good authority, and his testimony corroborated the statements of Mr. Tappan, and aided the friends of 'pure wine.' "[21]

Eventually an increasing number of evangelical churches switched over to the use of grape juice for communion, beginning with the New School Presbyterians and finally including almost all the post-Reformation Protestant denominations in the United States. However, Arthur soon discovered that those to whom drinking or drunkenness was a way of life were not so easily won over by a tasty functional substitute. The next logical step, in his mind, was forced legal abstinence — prohibition. "If men could be persuaded to abandon hard drinking, he rejoiced in it," Lewis recalls, but if they would, in spite of remonstrance and entreaty, become drunkards, he was decidedly for prohibiting the distillation and sale of the article that enabled them to destroy body and soul. It is lawful for a legislature to prohibit the sale of poisons. Intoxicating drinks are poisons, and therefore it is right that they should be prohibited."[22] Prohibition began to be urged by the American

Temperance Union on the local, state, and later national level. Maine was the first state to respond, prohibiting by law the sale of intoxicants in 1851.

As in most of the Tappans' reforming efforts, Arthur was more public in his involvement. Lewis, however, was also greatly interested and involved in temperance reform. On February 23rd, 1836, he recorded in his journal that he attended one of a number of "simultaneous temperance meetings . . . to be held throughout the civilized world."[23] He gave a short speech there and recorded with satisfaction that forty-eight people signed a pledge of total abstinence from all intoxicating beverages. Nearly ten years later, still active in the cause, he was one of twenty-five American delegates to a World Temperance Convention (1846) held in London.

In addition to their involvement in the temperance movement, the Tappans were also a part of the world peace movement. The American Peace Society had been growing stronger since 1813; cooperation was high with the London Peace Society, dominated by the Society of Friends. The peace crusade was at its height of activity in both England and America between 1837 and 1851. Like the temperance and the anti-slavery movements, the peace movement had two large factions — those advocating complete pacifism and those advocating arbitration, but not complete pacifism. Those who advocated thoroughgoing pacifism were radical on the basis of principle — neither offensive or defensive war was acceptable. William Lloyd Garrison, the radical abolitionist, helped develop and propagate the doctrine of non-resistance, and in 1838 he and others broke off from the American Peace Society to form the New England Non-Resistance Society. Unlike the course taken in their temperance efforts, the Tappans sided with the more "practical" advocates of international arbitration, rather than carrying their principles to the extreme. A similar split occurred between the Tappans and Garrison at a later date over anti-slavery issues: Garrison being more radical in his fervent denunciation of slavery and slave holders.

The peace movement, like the temperance and anti-slavery movements, was drawn irresistibly from moral exhortation to political action. In the 1840's, the high point of moral insurgency against war was the League of Universal Brotherhood, whose members were required to sign a pledge of peace. But like other such pledges of good intentions, there was danger of loss of enthusiasm and relapse. To ensure peace, William Jay, President of the

American Peace Society and son of the John Jay who had helped work out the peace treaty with England at the close of the Revolutionary War, originated the idea of writing arbitration clauses into treaties. This idea proved more successful than the "American Plan" for a Congress of Nations. Jay's proposals were adopted by the American and London Peace Societies at the World Peace Convention of 1843, of which Lewis Tappan was the American vice-president. Although the peace movement languished in the 1850's with the onset of the Crimean War and the increasing controversy over slavery in America, it had been sufficiently adamant to achieve the insertion of an arbitration clause in the Treaty of Paris after the Crimean War.[24]

Perhaps the most problematic of all the reforming efforts of the Tappans other than their anti-slavery effort, was their attack on prostitution in New York City, made through the Magdalen Society. In the summer of 1831, the society published a report written by John McDowell giving a general account of Manhattan prostitution and "estimates of the extent of prevailing vice." McDowell estimated that in New York City some ten thousand women were engaged in the trade. Because the report exposed, with some degree of truth, the situation in the city, it was opposed by those whose interests were hurt; because the report was too explicit in some areas, it was opposed by evangelicals. As Lewis Tappan later recalled, the report "was received with a burst of indignation and with threats of vengeance."[25] With the exception of David Hale's evangelical *Journal of Commerce,* the city dailies loudly denounced Arthur Tappan, President of the Magdalen Society, and the other trustees for their wild statements.[26]

Although in writing the "Magdalen Report" Mr. McDowall "was not always so prudent and discreet as he should have been," Lewis was surprised and upset at the number of "professing Christians" that opposed it severely. "Mr. McDowall did as well as he could under the trying circumstances in which he was placed," Lewis argued. "He gathered the moral statistics of crime, and published them under the inspection and endorsement of two physicians, without fear of consequence . . . Let not his zeal, even if it trespassed sometimes on the borders of indiscretion, be severely censured."[27]

As president of the society, Arthur was threatened with personal violence. Having unwittingly fanned the fires of anti-evangelicalism, the Magdalen Society faced mounting opposition and pressure. The strongest reaction came from several leaders of Tammany Hall, whose hostility lasted for some time.* The opposition also included such powerful leaders as Theophilus Fisk, a Universalist minister and Democratic party pamphleteer; Francis Wright, the labor leader and free thinker; and Mordecai M. Noah, the distinguished Jewish newspaperman and playwright who had previously attested to the use of unfermented wine in the first century passover.[28] Within a year, the Magdalen Society had dissolved; Arthur claimed that "the true cause [of the dissolution] was the discouraging fact that we saw no fruits of our labors."[29] McDowall, feeling the surrender was due to pressure and financial difficulties, continued in his labors, preaching in the open streets of Five Points, a slum district, and circulating literature. Lewis attributed the failure to the pressure of the "wicked [who] feared exposure and the opposers of wickedness [who] were apprehensive that reformatory measures had been overdone." They had, he admitted, "unnerved a large majority of the Christian community."[30] The solution to the problem of prostitution and similar vices, both he and Arthur subsequently decided, must originate in solid Biblical teaching and sex education on the part of ministers and parents.[31] They continued, however, to personally support the work of McDowall until his premature death a few years later at age thirty-five.[32]

The degree of involvement and the variety of concerns demonstrated by the Tappan brothers cannot be easily covered. The positions that Arthur Tappan held at one time or another will, however, help to give an overview of their scope of activities. They include: President of the American Educational Society, Finance Chairman of the American Tract Society (which he helped to found in 1826), Manager of the American Bible Society, Auditor of the American Home Missionary Society, Life Director of the American Seamen's Friend Society and of the Society for Meliorating the Condition of the Jews, Treasurer of the Society for Promoting Common School Education in Greece, Trustee of the Mercantile Library Association, Secretary of the Sabbath Union, and first president of the Anti-Slavery Society. The Tappans were involved in both large international societies and small local societies. Their status or reputation does not appear to have been a matter of concern for them in choosing where to devote their time and energy. This fact, along with their amazing personal perseverance and

---

*For a discussion of political reasons, see Wyatt-Brown, *Lewis Tappan and the Evangelical War Against Slavery*, 68-9.

conviction, can perhaps be best seen in their anti-slavery efforts, to be covered in the next chapter.

NOTES

1. Benjamin P. Thomas, *Theodore Weld: Crusader for Freedom* (New Brunswick, 1950), 29.

2. Bertram Wyatt-Brown, *Lewis Tappan and the Evangelical War Against Slavery* (Cleveland, 1969), 53.

3. Thomas, *Op. Cit.,* 31.

4. New York *Evangelist,* April 23, 1831.

5. Thomas, *Op. Cit.,* 31.

6. Loc. Cit.

7. Wyatt-Brown, *Op. Cit.,* 54.

8. Thomas, *Op. Cit.,* 31.

9. Ibid., 18-19.

10. Quoted in Thomas, *Op. Cit.,* 19.

11. Thomas, *Op. Cit.,* 18.

12. Ibid., 25.

13. Ibid., 34, 39.

14. Wyatt-Brown, *Op. Cit.,* 50.

15. Ibid., 67.

16. Ibid., 66.

17. Ibid., 67.

18. Ibid., 66.

19. Lewis Tappan, *The Life of Arthur Tappan* (Westport, Conn., 1970 ed.), 104.

20. Ibid., 105.

21. Ibid.,

22. Ibid., 106-107.

23. Diary, February 23, 1836.

24. Frank Thistlethwaite, "The Anglo American World" in David Brion Davis, ed., *Ante-Bellum Reform* (New York, 1967), 81.

25. Tappan, *Op. Cit.,* 113.

26. Wyatt-Brown, *Op. Cit.,* 68.

27. Tappan, *Op. Cit.,* 114-115.

28. Wyatt-Brown, *Op. Cit.* 69.

29. Tappan, *Op. Cit.,* 118.

30. Ibid., 116.

31. Ibid., 120-122.

32. Ibid., 119.

8
The Anti-slavery Crusade

OF ALL THE reforming efforts made by the Tappans, the most prolonged, intense and costly was their effort to eradicate slavery from America. Their interest in the slavery issue began when, as young men, their mother had encouraged them to read of William Wilberforce's struggles in England to outlaw the foreign slave trade. The aged Wilberforce and Thomas Clarkson (two members of the famous evangelical activist group in Parliament known as the "Clapham Sect") led the British evangelicals from 1709 to 1830 in their agitation for Parliamentary abolition of slavery in the West Indies. As the agitation in England grew, the Tappans and other New York philanthropists began to feel convicted that American slavery was not being effectively assailed. Theodore Weld began to turn from his interests in temperance and manual labor reform to the problem of slavery. He was influenced through his regular correspondence with his friend and idol, Charles Stuart, who had gone to England to help in the anti-slavery efforts there. The Tappans, in turn, were inspired by Theodore Weld, and through some direct correspondence with Wilberforce.[1]

In 1827 Arthur Tappan joined the American Colonization Society, founded in 1816. On the premise that even in freedom the blacks would at best lead a meager existence in America, the American Colonization Society proposed that blacks be freed and transported to Africa. To meet this goal, the Society founded the colony of Liberia — following a British prototype in Sierra Leone, which was supposed to be doing well under evangelical Christianity and British colonial control. Charles Tappan, brother of Lewis and Arthur, was especially active in this venture, and arranged in 1828 for his brothers to handle the majority of Liberian exports and shipping. In addition, Arthur accepted the vice-presidency of the African Education Society, a subsidiary of the American Colonization Society.[2]

Arthur and Lewis soon became disillusioned, however, with the Colonization Society's plans, and withdrew their membership late in 1831. Their motives for doing so involved several distinct issues. The commercial enterprise they had planned with the colony fell through when their contact in Liberia died of tropical fever. According to their own accounts, however, there were other issues which were much more influential in changing their opinions. Arthur had discovered that New England rum was Liberia's major import, and that its other imports included power and shot and weapons of war. The Society's aid in such matters and their refusal to prohibit "the admission of ardent spirits into the colony" shook Arthur's confidence in the principles and Christian basis of the Society.[3] About the same time Arthur began to read the arguments of William Lloyd Garrison in *The Liberator* and was persuaded that ridding America of free slaves would help to strengthen, rather than undermine, the system of slavery.[4] Arthur himself had bailed Garrison out of jail a few years before and had helped financially to start his anti-slavery newspaper, *The Liberator*.

In his book on Arthur, Lewis emphasized other points that distressed them about the American Colonization Society. He pointed out that in talking with some free blacks, they discovered that these blacks did not want to go to a foreign and primitive colony. To force them to choose expatriation was no better, Lewis concluded, than slavery itself.[5] While the Colonization Society claimed that the freed slaves could " 'never . . . be elevated here to equal rights, and will ever be unhappy and miserable while they remain among us,' " Lewis responded, "This, if true, . . . is our fault and not theirs. We are bound to remove obstacles, to give the colored man a chance, offer him the right hand of fellowship, do away with oppressive enactments and usages, treat him as a fellow-citizen, and fellow-Christian, *here,* in the land of his nativity. Christ died for the colored man as well as for the white man. He is no respecter of persons."[6]

The fact that Christ was "no respecter of persons" — that is, did not treat people differently according to their status — influenced Lewis to take that attitude as his own goal. In 1836, he stated in the New York *Evangelist:* I am for treating our colored brethren thus — *try to forget they are colored and act accordingly.* This seems to be imitating Christ of whom it was said 'Thou regardest not the persons of men' . . . If ye fulfill the royal law, according to scripture, thou shalt love thy neighbor (thy colored brother) as thyself."[7] With this conviction, Lewis worked to get the evangelical churches to integrate their seating. Finney, at Chatham Street Chapel, argued that people were not ready for that yet, and it could not be enforced by the church leadership. He went on to say that even "forty of the best men in the city could not be forced to practice that of associating in churches with people of color."[8] Unable to persuade the church at large and feeling that he at least must live by his principles, Lewis began to sit in the black section of the church. Such a move did not go unnoticed — he was rebuked from all sides. In frustration, he decided, "As Christians — and Christian abolitionists — will not tolerate my associating with my colored brethren in a white man's ch(urc)h it seems my duty to unite with a colored ch(urc)h. But," he wondered, "will it not invite insult to my col(ore)d brethren? I have prayed to the Lord this evening for guidance. . ."[9] A week later he wrote, "I do not know but this is the way to conquer prejudice in the community."[10] Apparently, he eventually decided on a middle course, attending both churches part time.

In June 1831, Arthur Tappan had met a young Congregational minister, Simeon S. Jocelyn, during the First Annual Convention of People of Color in Philadelphia. Jocelyn, who served a black church in New Haven, had come up with a plan for a Negro training school to be located near Yale College. The convention applauded Jocelyn's idea — one of the first means of advancement offered to the black race in America (rather than simply free transportation to an African outpost).[11] Arthur was enthusiastic about the idea due to the high value he placed on moral and utilitarian instruction. The plans went ahead. Arthur bought choice acres near Yale, expecting a few Yale professors to be willing to offer their services at a nominal cost. Garrison was delighted with the proposal and progress. "The offer made by Mr. Tappan is characteristic of his generosity. What a faithful steward of the Lord!" Garrison exclaimed. "His heart is a perpetual fountain of benevolence, which waters the whole land . . ."[12] A convention with fifteen delegates from five states was held to discuss the college. Both Lewis and Arthur addressed the convention. It was agreed for the "colored people to raise $10,000 ($300,000) and the whites to raise a similar sum. There are to be seven trustees of the College (four of them colored) to be chosen by the subscribers to the institution."[13]

Unfortunately, the plan turned out to be ill-fated. In late August 1831, fifty-five whites lost their lives in a slave uprising led by Nat Turner in Southampton County, Virginia. The uprising was brutally and quickly suppressed. Without a reasonable basis, citizens blamed Garrison and his *Liberator* for stirring slave rebellion.[14] Arthur offered him one thousand dollars for legal defense. Although that did not prove necessary, the plans for the black college were wrecked. Seven hundred citizens staged a rally in New Haven, Connecticut to protest it; no professors from Yale sided with Jocelyn and the Tappans. An angry mob attacked Arthur's house, breaking windows and cursing both anti-slavery and the Magdalen Society. "As riots and subtler signs of fear and scorn swirled about them, abolitionists, it seemed, were correct in attacking the slave system and racial prejudice as national, not sectional, tragedies."[15] One of Arthur's daughters had died during the Magdalen crisis, and he had incurred enough criticism for himself and his family for the while. Feeling that it would be fool-hardy to attempt to start over at this point, Arthur withdrew from the plan.

In the meantime, Garrison had begun promulgating the doctrine of "immediate abolition." As one historian put it: "The movement for 'immediate abolition' began as a direct extension of evangelical Christianity."[16] Garrison's arguments were stated in the columns of *The Liberator*. A basic evangelical belief was that sin was a conscious, active disobedience of God. Sin required a conversion of repentance, and change in action. One did not compromise with sin, or accept half-hearted repentance. Garrison carried this perspective over into his attack on slavery by arguing that, in God's eyes, it was surely a sin to condone or promote slavery. As in the revivalistic experiences, people needed to be converted, religiously, not secularly, to this spiritual doctrine. "The 'plan' which abolitionists proposed [therefore] was merely 'to promulgate the doctrine' of immediate abolition, leaving its actual accomplishment in the hands of those consciences they touched . . . They were not more unreasonable in preaching immediacy than a preacher who refused to advocate 'the gradual abolition of sin.' Immediate emancipation was not radical or silly . . . since any other proposal encouraged the universal inclination of men to procrastinate."[17]

By putting forth the doctrine of "immediate abolition," the evangelical abolitionists neither hoped for the whole nation to immediately convert, nor did they intend it as a plan of political action. In a manner very similar to those used in the revivals, they hoped to "convert" people, as individuals, to their way of thinking. To convert them to anything *less* than the ideal seemed unreasonable. The use of physical force to achieve their goals did not cross their minds (no more than the evangelists would have considered "converting" people to Christ at gun point or by law).

At one point, Joshua Leavitt, the editor of the New York *Evangelist,* tried to push the anti-slavery movement into the political arena. He proposed that a political party be formed with forced legal abolition as one of its platforms. One historian records: ". . . the whole body of abolitionists condemned his 'monstrous suggestion . . . that a religious society [the American Anti-Slavery Society] should . . . seek to build up political parties on geographical distinctions, and to array one section of the country against another.' Even the New York Committee reproved him, and Lewis Tappan published a condemnation of his course."[18] Regarding this "Liberty Party," Lewis Tappan wrote to a friend: "From the commencement of this movement I have thought it would lead abolitionists away from the moral and religious aspects of the cause, and induce them in party conflicts that would prove unfriendly to the progress of the anti-Slavery cause among the great body of religious men."[19]

The anti-slavery crusade was seen to be primarily a moral and religious concern. Basic to the abolitionists' methods was a sincere belief that men, upon being clearly presented with the truth, would not hesitate to accept it and change their ways. " 'Let the information be circulated,' Garrison reasoned concerning slavery, 'and Americans cannot long act and reason as they do.' "[20] This evangelical attitude — that providing correct information would result in people making correct decisions — pervaded evangelical thought in all areas. As one historian points out: "Evangelicals were convinced that any man, properly instructed, could see the superiority of the Christian system. They therefore emphasized the importance of education at all levels. The Sunday-School movement, originally designed to teach the poor to read, had as its rationale the assumption that the primary reading materials would be the Bible and the myriad evangelical tracts. Evangelicals encouraged also the establishment of elementary schools in the new settlements . . . Colleges were more crucial . . . In 1839, of the presidents of the fifty-four oldest colleges in the nation, fifty-one were clergymen, of these forty were Presbyterian."[21]

In the area of anti-slavery, therefore, the Tappans viewed education as an important means to accomplishing their goals. Earlier they had helped set up the evangelical Lane Seminary in Cincinnati, getting Lyman Beecher to accept the presidency. Then in March 1834, Theodore Weld, who had enrolled as a student there, staged an eighteen-day "protracted meeting" on the subject of slavery. These prayer and sermon sessions, handled much like debates, resulted in nearly all of the students, many Southerners included, being converted to "immediate abolitionism." Beecher, though himself a colonizationalist, tried to keep peace between the students and the conservative governing board. However, while he was on a trip to the East, the board, incensed by the work the students were doing among the free blacks in Cincinnati, threatened to expel those who did not give up their association with blacks. Beecher, who was trying to reconcile the "colonists" and the "immediate abolitionist" (to whose side the Tappans had already defected) tried to stand the middle ground. Arthur began then to look for a new site on which to establish an evangelical college with anti-slavery principles, to which these students could go. In 1835 the Tappans initiated the founding of Oberlin College in Ohio with Charles Finney to head up the Department of Theology; Arthur promised to ensure his salary. In the first year, Arthur donated over $7,000 ($210,000), lending an additional $10,000 ($300,000). Oberlin adopted the manual labor system of education, and became the first American school to let in both women and blacks. Soon Oberlin became the center of Western abolitionism, with its students acting as anti-slavery agents: distributing tracts, working with blacks, and giving anti-slavery lecture series in Western towns. Weld was extremely influential in this capacity.[22]

The Tappans had continued to be active in New York City as well. Recovering from the defeat of their plans for a black college, they pushed for the organization of a national anti-slavery society. Despite warnings from other anti-slavery societies that the American public was not ready to support a national society, they determined to go ahead with plans for a national convention.[23] On October 2nd, 1833, when the New York convention was scheduled to begin, mobs, fearing the outcome of such an organization, congregated outside of Tammany Hall. Arthur considered postponing the meeting, but Lewis insisted that they proceed on schedule — with one exception, that the location be changed from Clinton Hall to the Chatham Street Chapel. The news was quickly spread by word of mouth to the conventioneers. Meanwhile, some colonizationists and others opposed posted notices urging "patriots" to gather at Clinton Hall that night. When the mob reached the hall that evening, they found it deserted. In the nearby chapel, the abolitionists quickly adopted a constitution and elected officers. Arthur Tappan was chosen as president of the new New York Anti-Slavery Society. "Just then the rioters were heard storming up the street . . . Cries of 'Garrison, Garrison, Tappan, Tappan, where are they, find them, find them' filled the old theater."[24] The lights were quickly quenched within the chapel and the reformers scattered. Lewis and Arthur fled out the back door, evading a tipsy rioter with a lantern and dagger.

The national convention was held on December 4, 1833, gathering in Philadelphia to avoid the New York mobs. At the height of the meeting, after a speech given by Lewis Tappan, Garrison presented his "Declaration of Sentiments."The male participants signed the Declaration — to them an occasion echoing the signing of the Declaration of Independence. In it Garrison rejected "the use of all carnal weapons," instead looked to the doctrine that all men are created in equality, opposed compensation of slave-owners on the grounds of the immorality (and therefore nullity) of any claim to ownership of another man, and admitted that the system was under state and individual control, not national. (He urged Congressional authority in the Federal District, however, and — by means of the commerce clause — in interstate trade.)[25] Though not present, Arthur Tappan, the most distinguished and wealthy abolitionist, was elected president. Garrison, the only non-New Yorker among the national officers, became the secretary of foreign correspondence. He published the British endorsement of the American Anti-Slavery Society in *The Liberator:* "The excellent Constitution you have adopted, and the judicious choice of your officers, with that indefatigably devoted, great and good man, *Arthur Tappan* as your president . . . give assurance that you must conquer."[26] The society decided that most of its influence would be gained through the persuasive efforts of orators working among grass-roots evangelicals. Arthur entrusted Theodore Weld and Charles Finney with this task.

Meanwhile, Lewis took charge of the local New York situation. In the spring of 1834, Lewis organized an anti-slavery week to coincide with the spring shopping of country merchants in the city. Many country evangelicals attended the so-called "Holy Week" during which Lewis interviewed a black man — just back from Liberia — about the colonization proposal. The packed crowd at Chatham Street Chapel heard the sensational but matter-of-fact replies about rum-drunking, slave-trading, and conditions of health and religion "in the colony. Members of the National Colonization Society interrupted and accused the two of collusion."[27]

The following month anti-abolitionist slanders circulated by the press created an uproar in the city. "Unemployment was increasing rapidly, being estimated at ⅛ of the population in 1833. Fear of Negro competition in the labor market had as much to do with antislavery reform as did the intermarriage issue . . . Prejudice, not disapproval of immediate abolition as such, was the real cause of the rioting that followed, in which Negroes, more than their white friends, were the victims of terrible pillage and destruction."[28] On July 4th, 1834, rioters interrupted a special black service in Chatham Street Chapel being held in commemoration of New York State Emancipation Day. The service had been intended as a Christian alternative to the usual alcohol-infested celebrating going on in other parts of the city. Police dispelled the rioters before much damage was done. Three days later, however, a mob congregated in front of Lewis' new home on Rose Street in a quiet middle-class neighborhood, yelling for him to come out. Once more dispersed by the police, the mob returned the next night after Lewis had removed his family to another part of town. They smashed the doors and windows, hurled the furniture out into the street, and burned furniture, bedding, pictures, and window frames in a hugh bonfire. Lewis wryly noted in his journal that they "needed a bigger house anyway."[29] His wife, seeing that a large chimney glass (which for eighteen years Lewis had proclaimed to be too extravagant) was destroyed, laughed and told him, "You have got rid of that piece of furniture that troubled you so much whenever we had prayer meetings in that room."[30] Lewis proudly reported his wife's uncomplaining attitude to Weld. The New York *Courier* and the *Enquirer*, always antagonistic to the Tappans, reported that only one window had been broken while a group of gentlemen demonstrated peacefully — others commended the rioters for their civil spirit. But Lewis left his home unrepaired for the rest of the summer of 1834 to serve as a "silent Anti-Slavery preacher to the crowds who will flock to see it."[31] On following days, the mobs attacked churches of evangelical abolitionists and of the free blacks. One of the "free churches" that Lewis had helped start, the Presbyterian Church on Spring Street, was attacked. Barricades were set up to delay police; the rioters smashed doors and windows, entered and demolished the organ, pulpit and pews. A troop of cavalry intervened as the mob was tearing down the balcony.[32] The American Anti-Slavery Society tried, unsuccessfully, to prove their good intentions by publishing a disclaimer to counteract the slander of other papers, publishing as well their Constitution and Declaration of Sentiments to show that they had no subversive or violent goals.

Between 1835 and 1836, in an effort to gain more members and greater public acceptance, the Tappans and a few friends staged for the American Anti-Slavery Society what one historian calls "the great postal campaign."[33] At the second annual meeting (in 1835) Lewis Tappan had proposed to the American Anti-Slavery Society a budget of $60,000 ($1.8 million) for the coming year for a national pamphlet campaign. As chairman of the publications committee, Lewis outlined his plan. A series of four journals would be issued each month (one per week): first, *Human Rights,* a four page sheet; second, the *Anti-Slavery Record,* embellished with woodcuts; third, the *Emancipator,* no longer a weekly but enlivened a bit; fourth, *The Slave's Friend,* to be geared toward young people. These papers would then be sent to community leaders all over the nation. All abolitionists were encouraged to participate in their distribution. Women were encouraged to cover pincushions and workboxes to produce funds for the great campaign. The leaders of the some 200 small local anti-slavery associations sent in "names of 'inquiring, candid, reading men who were not abolitionists' to whom the new materials would be sent by direct mail."[34] The rest of the literature would be distributed by the local associations to interested citizens.

Lewis Tappan, already experienced in editing and publication, helped Elizur Wright put out *Human Rights* and prepared *The Slave's Friend* himself. Twenty-five to fifty thousand copies were printed and distributed each week. Although nation-wide coverage was their goal, much of the literature was geared toward northern churchgoers and typical working-class Yankees. By creating a wave of excitement and awareness, they hoped to turn the tide of public sentiment until it was generally against slavery. Southern resistance would then prove hopeless in the face of national and international rebuke. In the face of powerful social pressure, the slave-holders, Lewis Tappan reasoned, would surrender peaceably. Violence would exist, he admitted, but would be only a passing phase.[35]

Before the Society's next anniversary, in May 1836, Lewis Tappan's publication board had issued over a million anti-slavery pieces. Although violent reactions had been expected, the degree of violence demonstrated by the Southerners took Lewis Tappan and his friends by surprise. On July 29, 1835, a group of "patriotic" Charlestonians broke into the U.S. Post Office, stealing the anti-slavery mail bags. The following evening, 3,000 Charlestonians watched as Arthur Tappan, Garrison, and Samuel H. Cox (a New York evangelical minister) were hung in effigy while the abolitionist papers were burned below them. Public protest meetings were held, circulars were issued; the postmaster general was asked to overlook the Southern violation of the mails as they sought to intercept all anti-slavery materials entering the state. In the free states, mail censorship laws were demanded. "Hitherto, the South had considered antislavery more a future than a present danger, but suddenly fears of national intervention were alive, and forecasts of disastrous consequences filled the newspaper columns. . . . For the first time in the Tappan's experience, . . . the real danger was not from local bullies but from the South."[36]

Arthur Tappan received the brunt of the critics' blows. In East Feliciana, Louisiana a rally pledged a $30,000 ($900,000) reward for the delivery of Arthur to the New Orleans wharf. The Rev. J.C. Postell of South Carolina raised $100,000 ($3,000,000) if Arthur Tappan and La Roy Sunderland (a Methodist abolitionist editor) were brought to the South. "When asked about these tempting prizes, Arthur is said to have replied in a . . . brave moment of humor, 'If that sum is placed in a New York bank, I may possibly think of giving myself up.' "[37] Threats of this kind added to the publicity of anti-slavery, and the August, 1835 issue of *Human Rights* pointed out that "Nothing is really anti-abolitionist, but apathy." But violence was just below the surface. One abolitionist claimed that someone at the Merchant's Exchange, just across the street from Arthur Tappan & Company, had announced a bid of $5,000 ($150,000) for Arthur's head. The mayor of Brooklyn considered the danger real enough to have the front of Arthur's house patrolled regularly and to station a relay of men at the Brooklyn Navy Yard in case military force became necessary.[38] The riots of 1834 had ensured safe-keeping to the Tappans since the City, having had to severely put down the riots after they had spread to the attacking of non-abolitionist people, churches and stores, wanted no repeat of the contagious mob violence.

While Garrison gloried in his infamy, practically hoping to be blessed with martyrdom, Arthur was not so enthusiastic about the progressively worsening state of affairs. The South managed to organize an economic campaign against Arthur's company, which sold much of its silk goods in the South. Beginning in Charleston, storekeepers were urged to halt all trade with the Tappans. The boycott spread quickly. One historian notes, "It must have been one of the first organized attempts to bankrupt a national business because of its owners' political and moral convictions."[39] This boycott not stopping the Tappans, the Charleston activists urged the South to move toward a boycott of all New York City goods. As one historian records, "In late August and September 1835 a non-importation movement against the whole city was discernable . . . the Southern economic plan . . . was enough to excite the fears of New York businessmen."[40] The leading men of New York were soon pressuring Arthur to stop his anti-slavery activities. Lewis records that in response to a delegation from the Chamber of Commerce (in spite of the "peculiar responsibility" Arthur felt to "his creditors, his partners and his family") he stated, "You demand that I shall cease my anti-slavery labors . . . . – *I will be hung first!*"[41]

As the South became more violent, "lynch law" went into effect. Innocent people were being hung or burned alive in Southern states. In 1837, E.P. Lovejoy, a Presbyterian anti-slavery publisher in Alton, Illinois, was shot to death. Although he was later acclaimed a martyr for the cause, the pacifistic abolitionists were shocked to discover that he had been keeping arms in his office. Weld's sister-in-law, Sarah Grimké, lamented: "And E.P. Lovejoy keeping arms in his office! Truly I fear we have yet to learn the lesson 'Trust in the Lord' . . . Surely posterity will brand us hypocrites." Garrison called it a "dangerous precedent." Angelina Grimké, Weld's wife, went further in demonstrating her pacifist sentiments when she expressed the hope "that our blood will be spilt instead of the slave holders'; our lives will be taken, and theirs spared."[42]

The postal campaign catapulted abolition into the political arena at the next session of Congress in December 1836. Amos Kendall, the postmaster-general, had already virtually endorsed state postal inspection. Now, in his annual message to Congress, "[President Andrew] Jackson, that alleged champion of American liberty, requested the passage of a national censorship law to prohibit the dissemination of dangerous writings."[43] Although this law was never passed, the anti-slavery issue had been recognized and debated on the floor of Congress. Beginning in 1836, near the end of the great postal campaign, John Quincy Adams steadily introduced anti-slavery materials to the House of Representatives, in spite of the bipartisan passage of "gag" rules.

In the meantime, the number of anti-slavery societies had more than doubled, and 15,000 people had subscribed to the Society's publication in the course of the year, possibly (as one historian suggests) a growth unparalleled in the history of reform.[44]

Nevertheless, the American Anti-Slavery Society began facing financial difficulties, due to the rising opposition and a shaky national economy resulting from the panic caused when Jackson withdrew U.S. treasury funds from the Bank of the United States. Arthur Tappan, personally responsible for all debts incurred by the unincorporated Society, tried to hold its expenses within the bounds of its income. In October 1839, the Society was in desperate financial shape. Lewis Tappan called a meeting at Cleveland with local societies, but they refused to offer financial support.

Things were not going well in other areas of the society's life. The American Anti-Slavery Society was splitting down the center, with the Tappans and the New Yorkers on one side and the Garrisonians on the other. "The *Liberator* was turning increasingly from denouncing slavery to denouncing slave-holders. Through its circulation in the South, Arthur, as president of the Society, had become increasingly hated; rewards were being offered for his capture. In New Orleans $20,000 ($600,000) was offered publicly "for his person."[45] The Tappans objected to Garrison's inflammatory measures; Arthur asked for his name to be removed from the *Liberator's* acknowledgments. When Garrison, again in financial trouble, applied for aid from the New York Committee for his paper, he was flatly refused. Lewis tried to mediate at first, urging Garrison to write more temperately.[46]

Finney, meanwhile, was urging the Tappans to realize that unless reforms such as abolition were introduced *after* a true spiritual conversion, they would neither be heard nor effective. "Denunciation would serve the cause, he said, only as it was uttered in a spirit of loving reproof. But denunciation in a censorous spirit such as he was now hearing, would carry the nation 'fast into a civil war. Unless the public mind can be engrossed with the subject of salvation, and make abolitionism an appendage . . . the church and world, ecclesiastical and state leaders, will become embroiled in one common infernal squabble that will roll a wave of blood over the land.' "[47] In teaching his students at Oberlin, Finney emphasized that the cause of Christ must come first — that "unconverted masters will be oppressors still." The Tappans, in return, considered Finney a traitor to the anti-slavery cause, "who was 'sinning against conscience' by his refusal to pray for abolition in public."[48] Arthur, however, continued to support Oberlin. Lewis' discouragement over the misunderstanding is recorded in his journal: "It is a lamentable thing to have a falling out with so good a man as br(other) Finney and I hope I did not do wrong."[49]

In Boston, two older Tappan brothers, also of orthodox persuasion, chose another route in an attempt to avoid the gathering tragedy. In consultation with General John H. Cocke, an aristocratic slaveholder whom John Tappan had met through common temperance interests and one of the last of the Southern liberals opposed to slavery, John and Charles Tappan issued a call for the formation of "The American Union for the Relief and Improvement of the Colored People." John Tappan was quite wealthy and well-respected. Gustave de Beaumont, when visiting Boston with Alexis de Toqueville, had said of John, "I declare I have never met anyone whose character and virtues inspired in me a more profound respect."[50] In establishing the American Union in 1835, the brothers hoped to draw Southern evangelicals back into the discussion and action. Garrison denounced the apologetic spirit of the new organization, while Arthur endorsed it and hoped that the two organizations could work together in a spirit of brotherhood. "Mr. Garrison," he wrote in the Boston *Recorder*, "had the fault of using 'severe and denunciatory language with which he often assails his opponents and repels their attacks.' "[51]

In such a state of dissension, the American Anti-Slavery Society could not last long. In 1840, the New York board met and decided to disband the organization. An article appeared in the *Emancipator* March 26, 1840: "To the members of the American Anti-Slavery Society . . . Believing, then, that the American Anti-Slavery Society is no longer necessary for the advancement of the Anti-Slavery cause — but rather (owing to our dissensions) a hindrance, bringing the whole anti-Slavery movement into disrepute, it is proposed for your serious consideration, whether THE SOCIETY OUGHT NOT TO BE FORMALLY DISSOLVED."[52]

The American Anti-Slavery Society had not gone down without making its impact on the national scene — an impact that, though led by the Tappans' financial and managerial powers, ironically changed the course of the anti-slavery movement towards violence and political action — the very direction that they so vehemently wished to avoid. Charles Finney's prophetic words, then, were to come to pass as the greatest of the Tappans' reforming efforts was wrenched out of their hands, grew uncontrollable in its size and violence, and rolled "a wave of blood over the land."

NOTES

1. Lewis Tappan, *The Life of Arthur Tappan* (Westport, Conn., 1970 ed.), 126.
2. Bertram Wyatt-Brown, *Lewis Tappan and the Evangelical War Against Slavery* (Cleveland, 1969), 86.
3. Letter from Arthur Tappan to Lewis Laine, quoted from Tappan, *Op. Cit.*, 129.
4. Loc. Cit.
5. Tappan, *Op. Cit.*, 127.
6. Ibid., 123.
7. New York *Evangelist*, March 24, 1836.
8. Dairy, February 25, 1836.
9. Diary, February 26, 1836.
10. Diary, March 3, 1836.
11. Wyatt-Brown, *Op. Cit.*, 87.
12. Walter Merrill, ed., *The Letters of William Lloyd Garrison, 1822-1835,* Vol. I, II, & III (Cambridge, Mass., 1971), 47.
13. Ibid., 49.
14. Waytt-Brown, *Op. Cit.*, 32.
15. Ibid., 89.
16. Ibid., 81.
17. Ibid., 82.
18. Gilbert H. Barnes, *The Anti-Slavery Impulse 1830-1844* (New York, 1933), 164.
19. Letter to Gerrit Smith, September 9, 1843.
20. Wyatt-Brown, *Op. Cit.*, 110.
21. George M. Marsden, *The Evangelical Mind and the New School Presbyterian Experience – A Case Study in Thought and Theology in Nineteenth-Century America* (New Haven, 1970), 30.
22. Wyatt-Brown, *Op. Cit.*, 131.
23. Alice Felt Tyler, *Freedom's Ferment: Phases of American Social History from the Colonial Period to the Outbreak of the Civil War* (New York, 1944), 492.
24. Wyatt-Brown, *Op. Cit.*, 105.
25. Ibid., 108.
26. *Liberator*, April 12, 1834.
27. Wyatt-Brown, *Op. Cit.*, 116.
28. Ibid., 160.
29. Diary, Mary 22, 1836.
30. Lewis Tappan to Theodore Weld, July 10, 1834.
31. Tappan, *Op. Cit.*, 208; Wyatt-Brown, *Op. Cit.*, 118.
32. Tappan, *Op Cit.*, 213.
33. Wyatt-Brown, *Op. Cit.*, 149.
34. Ibid., 143.
35. Ibid., 143-145.
36. Ibid., 150-151.
37. Ibid., 152.
38. Tappan, *Op. Cit.*, 249-250.
39. Wyatt-Brown, *Op. Cit.*, 155.

40. Ibid., 156.
41. Tappan, *Op. Cit.*, 269.
42. Merrill, *Op. Cit.*, 212.
43. Wyatt-Brown, *Op. Cit.*, 162.
44. Ibid., 163.
45. Merrill, *Op. Cit.*, 207.
46. *Wyatt-Brown, Op. Cit.*, 134.
47. Barnes, *Op. Cit.*, 162.
48. Ibid., xxviii.
49. Diary, March 19, 1836.
50. Wyatt-Brown, *Op. Cit.*, 134.
51. Ibid., 139.
52. Newspaper clipping in Diary of Lewis Tappan, March 26, 1840 taken from *Emancipator*, March 26, 1840.

9

An Inside Look

THE GREAT fury of activity in which the Tappans were continually involved gives at least a surface indication of their view of reform. They were enthusiastic and urgent; they demonstrated perseverance and a somewhat rigid determination to reach their goals. Obviously, reforms of great number and variety were important to them; equally important was their desire to be personally involved — either actively or merely financially — in those reforms.

Taking a deeper look into the personal motives behind their reforming efforts will inevitably be more subjective and less accurate. An evaluation from the distance of the twentieth century will tend to be distorted with biases indigenous to this period. Nevertheless, it is important to attempt investigation into motives powerful enough to lead the Tappans to risk families, businesses, and even their own lives in pursuit of reform.

Perhaps the most unbiased view can be had through a look at the Tappans' own recorded perceptions and motivations. By accepting as valid their self-admitted motives, by avoiding the tendency to impute hidden motives or unknown neuroses to their activities, a fairly clear analysis may be developed regarding the inward values which so forcefully drove the Tappans toward zealous and untiring reform.

The Tappan brothers (as is the case with most people) did not regularly discuss at length and in detail the reasons behind their actions. To them, most of what they did must have seemed the obvious course of action. However, quite a few times friends, or others, called them to give an account for their actions or explain their decisions. It is in these conflicts in relationships, then, that the most insight can be obtained. The possible tendency in such situations could have been to rationalize and justify their actions instead of stating their true reasons for doing what they did. But the truth of their explanations may be checked by noting the consistency in their statements to many different people. Because of their influential social positions, they were in contact with many people of quite a variety of opinions. At various times they had to explain themselves to evangelical family members, non-Christian family, revival leaders (such as Finney and Beecher), radical reformers (such as Garrison), liberal Christians, foreign Christian leaders, civil authorities, the general public, and angry mobs. The consistency in their explanations indicates the extent to which they reflected their true motivations.

Some of the misunderstandings which they had with other people and which elicited their explanations of their motivation have already been discussed, at least in part, in the preceding chapters. Rather than reviewing them in their entirety, the main points of disagreement will be re-emphasized, and a deeper look taken into the reasons and motives recorded by the Tappans in trying to bring about a reconciliation or understanding.

Starting "closest to home," one immediately encounters Lewis' lifelong debate with his deistic brother Benjamin over religious and reforming issues. In talking to his brother he emphasized that, in spite of any difference of opinion they may have had, in the last analysis they were each directly responsible to God: ". . . I quarrel with no man, or dislike him, for entertaining adverse principles," Lewis wrote Benjamin. "To his own master each and all must stand or fall. We are too weak and fallible to sit in judgment upon fellow-men."[1] Lewis did not view his attempts to convert Benjamin or others as a judgment of them or a quarrel with them. Instead, he felt constrained to evangelize as his joyous responsibility to spread the gospel ("good news") that Christ had entrusted to his followers.

In 1842 he wrote to his orthodox brother John, after some conflict over anti-slavery procedures: ". . . let us watch over our hearts, and pray much that they may be sanctified, and that all our faculties of mind and body may be consecrated to the Lord. So far as we can, let us think alike and act alike, but where we do not do this let us not slander one another nor advise one another, and most of all do not let us misrepresent the gospel of our divine Lord. If we have not his spirit we are none of his."[2]

The responsibility to follow Christ closely and carry out his commands was basic to the Tappans' faith and convictions. Life, as they viewed it, was a stewardship. All areas of one's life would be reviewed on the judgment day and evaluated with Christ as the standard. Although salvation was not the result of one's deeds, the sincerity of one's faith and love for God was demonstrated by the determination with which he strove for perfect obedience. Lewis continued in his letter to John, saying, "That you and I may possess it]Christ's spirit] a hundred fold more than we ever have done, that we may not only embrace the truth on all subjects, but courageously act out our convictions with reference to the judgment day, is the prayer of your ever affectionately obliged brother, Lewis Tappan."[3]

The process of serving God, then, they saw to be two-fold: first, seeking out the truth on all subjects and, secondly, courageously acting out one's convictions. If one *truly* believed something was the truth, there was no valid alternative, they reasoned, to a radical commitment to that principle, and action on that basis. Non-action was, therefore, often considered to be a sign of disbelief or concealed opposition rather than a result of ignorance. Anyone, they reasoned, with true interest and concern would not remain in apathetic ignorance. "Depend upon it," Lewis writes from experience to his English friend S.H. Mott in 1843, "there is as much fanaticism in lukewarmness as in zeal."[4] It is this very "fanatical" lukewarmness which Lewis spent much of his reforming career trying to counteract. In 1836, after a year-long massive postal campaign, he had managed to gain the ear of most American leaders. Yet it was then that he discovered that the problem stemmed not from ignorance of the truth about the evils of slavery, but rather that people apparently did not *want* to know the truth. When approached with the documented facts and statistics of Theodore Weld's book *Slavery As It Is,* most people (even those from the North, including surprisingly, many Christians) refused to listen or actively sought to suppress the message. The Tappans had originally expected most to embrace the truth and join the cause, but in many areas, and in particular the South, the reaction to the postal campaign even reached the point of murderously destructive violence.

The Tappans' emphasis on seeking God's truth and then acting on conviction helps to explain their often serious "falling-outs" with fellow reformers as well as their ability to maintain basic good-will with these people in the midst of such conflicts. Two of their major conflicts occurred with William Lloyd Garrison and Charles Grandison Finney. As they began to object more and more to the words and actions of Garrison, they stopped supporting his paper (the *Liberator*) and started their own (the *Emancipator*) under Arthur's jurisdiction. Nevertheless, though he did not support Garrison's methods, Lewis still defended him against pro-slavery attackers. As he noted to his cousin Eliza Bigelow, "I had rather answer for the sins of Garrison than the editors of the N.Y. Observer."[5] Tappan admitted that Garrison's workers had "talent and industry" and that they spoke "a great deal of truth, although they seem to do it in a bad spirit, reminding me of a zealot of whom it was said: he served God as if the devil were in him."[6] When the New York committee disbanded the American Anti-Slavery Society, putting all its goods into scattered storage, Garrison and his followers revived it under his own banner. This forced Lewis Tappan and the New Yorkers into the reactionary measure of forming the American and Foreign Anti-Slavery Society. This second society sought to divert the coming violence with the South by refocusing issues on a more international plane — hoping thereby to heal relations with some of the Southerners.

In the midst of this intensified conflict, the Tappans and Garrison still did not cease in their respect for each other. Each recognized the other's sincere convictions and undying desire to work toward the freeing of the slaves. In 1870, after the Civil War and nearly forty years after they had first met, Garrison wrote to Lewis Tappan: "Be assured, I shall always very gratefully remember your early friendship, your generous hospitality, your courageous and whole-souled espousal of the Anti-Slavery cause, in the midst of trials serenely met and nobly endured. What ever may have been the unhappy causes which, at a later period, led to our estrangement, or at least to our different methods of acting for the deliverance of the oppressed, nothing shall blind me to the fact that, during the long protracted struggle, no one evinced greater zeal, persistency, and disinterestedness [unselfishness] in resting the immediate and total abolition of slavery than yourself."[7]

The Tappan's conflict with Charles Finney also led to different courses of action but not to an enduring estrangement. The Tappans felt that Finey's choice of emphasizing the preaching of Christ over social issues was an inconsistency in his Christian life. Since he was the head professor of theology at Oberlin College, and was widely respected among evangelicals, they also worried about the influence his stance would have. Lewis noted in his journal: "I lament having such a discordance with Mr. F(inney) whom I love and respect on many accounts, but I believe his views and practices on the S(lavery) question have done much injury and that the inculcation of them on students will be very injurious."[8] Among Finney's more unreasonable decisions (from the Tappans' perspective, knowing as they did of his personal abolitionist beliefs) was his unwillingness to pray for abolition in public. To Finney, this action would have diverted people's attention from the central issue of a personal relationship with God. To the Tappans, to avoid such public pleas for the cause of the slaves was "shunning to treat them as the gospel requires."[9] Yet Lewis later affirms in his journal, "Differing from br(other) Finney as I do on the slavery question, I love him for his many excellent qualities."[10] In the midst of this conflict Arthur continued to support Oberlin, and later Lewis encouraged and aided Finney in the writing and publication of his autobiography.

The Tappans felt that the confrontation they had with Finney was due to Finney's unwillingness to boldly act out his principles. Finney, however, felt that he *was* boldly acting out his principles — conversion to Christ being the *only* peaceful route to abolition and other reforms in man. Once the Tappans had become persuaded that a certain concern was crucial in Christ's mind, however, their responsibility to *act* on it became their central concern. In persuading others of the importance of a certain reform, they did not realize the path their own thinking had taken so as to lead others through the same process. The atrocities of slavery shocked them into action because of their deep conviction that, under God, the blacks were their brothers, and Christ himself was being grieved by the treatment they were receiving. Through exposing these atrocities and mistreatments, they were convinced that others would react as they had. They were surprised, therefore, when others who lacked their foundational view of Christ and the humanity of black slaves did not respond with like horror.

In spite of the problems they encountered in interaction with others, the Tappans continued to emphasize in their own lives a radical commitment to the principles they saw in the teachings of Christ. This commitment involved not only public and social matters, such as the anti-slavery campaign, but also was evident in their attitude toward personal matters, such as finances. In 1836 Lewis noted in his journal: "For myself I have solemnly vowed I would not lay up property for my family."[11] He went on to state that he, therefore, could not take up a new business, as he was being encouraged to do, until he could sell his old business "and see the way clear soon to dispose of our purchases."[12] In 1865 he demonstrated the same spirit when he wrote to Finney, offering to financially underwrite the first publication of his *Revival Lectures.* "With regard to the use of property, it is my daily inquiry 'Lord, what wilt Thou have me to do?' "[13]

The conflicts which arose from the Tappans' desire to radically act on their principles — in spite of the resultant costs and dangers— distressed them. Their distress stemmed not so much from differences in opinion with their "brothers in Christ" but from the unloving or unaccepting spirit that occasionally accompanied these differences. In a letter to his cousin Eliza, Lewis lamented, "I wish for universal toleration. Independence of thought, speech and action is what I would contend for . . . There are many persons who will express a doubt whether you are a Christian or sane or sober if you differ from them on theory or practice. This is much in vogue in Boston . . . Oh for freedom! Intellectual, moral, religious freedom. Oh, for the liberty where with Jesus Christ can make men free."[14]

It is rarely possible to thoroughly understand the motivations which cause some men to become great reformers. There may be anger at personal injustice suffered. There may be a sense of identification with the oppressed. Or it may be a certain type of personality looking for a cause which brings about reform. None of these seem truly to fit the Tappan brothers. They could have lived lives of ease and great wealth, respected by both the social and the business world, and honored by politicians. But they chose to give away millions of dollars for all sorts of causes, keeping for themselves and their families only what was necessary "to supply ourselves and families, in a decent manner, as becomes those professing Godliness."[15] They risked their social standing, being repeatedly vilified by the press, rioted against, their homes looted and burned, and having prices put on their heads. Fellow businessmen begged them to retreat from their reforming goals, lest they also suffer by living in the same city. Politicians were infuriated and only very reluctantly supported a few of their reforms. Perhaps hardest of all for the Tappans was the misunderstandings they suffered from Christian ministers, their own brothers, and other more radical reformers. Yet they persisted in their efforts. Why? Their reputation among men, even when their business depended on it, was not as important to them as their faithfulness to boldly live for God. Lewis risked the success of his Mercantile Agency by continuing his anti-slavery efforts. Arthur, offering to "hang first" before stopping his labor for this cause, eventually went bankrupt when the silk-wearing South boycotted his company. Their sense of responsibility for the slave stemmed initially from their sense of responsibility to God. The same was true of their other reforming concerns.

There were many reasons for their zeal. The earliest was, no doubt, the influence of their parents, but from a family of eleven children, only two became such ardent reformers. They associated with other reformers, but more often than not were themselves the prime movers. The French Revolution with its massacres of the wealthy and Napoleon's creeping encroachment on all of Europe had startled the world and alarmed the United States with his invasion of Mexico. There was a sense that the day of God's judgment was near. But there was coupled with this a sense that God had chosen America for a special purpose. No other nation on earth had such an enlightened constitution and was so relatively free to try out new ideas. Evangelicals also felt that as a consequence no other nation on earth was so responsible to bring about God's kingdom on earth. "Evangelicals and even respectable journalists who were in no way associated with the evangelicals felt that the end of the world might be coming with the end of Andrew Jackson's administration — because of the revolts in Europe and in Spanish America which they called 'abuse of power.' The evangelicals felt themselves in a race to convert the entire world before the deadline of Christ's return."[16]

There was also the ever present example of England. Starting in 1790, and directly as a result of the Evangelical Awakening, England had been undergoing a series of reforms, not the least of which was the abolition of slavery and the slave trade. Incredible as it might seem to the modern American, what happened in England was much better known in the American North than what happened in the American South. "This was partly because the British press was read widely in the U.S., and in the North and middle colonies, less was consequently known about the South than about England."[17] "The parliamentary debates in 1830 [on slavery] were printed on the front page of all the great daily newspapers. A New York newspaper implied that the U.S. would have to follow the British pattern or be considered 'the most despicable nation on the face of the earth.' "[18] There was a certain naive feeling that if abolition could be accomplished in England through parliamentary debate and public agitation, then surely also in America it could be accomplished without war. But the economic system of the South was much more dependent on slavery than the reformers imagined.

If one were to choose one thing, however, which described the foundation of the Tappans' motivations for reform, it would probably be their belief that all aspects of their personal lives were entrusted to them as a stewardship from God. Long after both Lewis and Arthur Tappan had ceased to be prime movers in many of the varied American reform movements, they still had this sense of responsibility and stewardship. In his late seventies, Lewis still sought "to use what remains in my hands for such objects as appear to be best for the cause of our Master and the good of souls."[19] Continuing in his letter to Charles Finney, also near the end of his life, he summed up his basic perspective: "The places that now know us, dear brother Finney, will soon know us no more. Let us work while the day lasts. May we have the wisdom and grace to fulfill our stewardship so that we shall be neither afraid nor ashamed to appear before our Lord . . ."[20]

NOTES

1. Lewis Tappan to Benjamin Tappan, March 14, 1828.
2. Lewis Tappan to John Tappan, October 3, 1842.
3. Loc. Cit.
4. Lewis Tappan to S.H. Mott, September 9, 1843.
5. Lewis Tappan to Eliza Bigelow, December 26, 1843.
6. As quoted by Bertram Wyatt-Brown, *Lewis Tappan and the Evangelical War Against Slavery* (Cleveland, 1969), 289.
7. William Lloyd Garrison to Lewis Tappan, January 27, 1870.
8. Diary, April 26, 1836.
9. Diary, March 19, 1836.
10. Diary, May 2, 1836.
11. Diary, March 18, 1836.
12. Loc. Cit.
13. Lewis Tappan to Charles Finney, April 24, 1865.
14. Lewis Tappan to Eliza Bigelow, January 14, 1844.
15. Gilbert H. Barnes, *The Anti-Slavery Impulse 1830-1844* (New York, 1933), 21.
16. Bernard A. Weisberger, *They Gathered at the River: The Story of Revivalists and Their Impact Upon Religion in America* (Boston, 1958), 131.
17. Barnes, *Op. Cit.*, 18.
18. Ibid., 29.
19. Lewis Tappan to Charles Finney, April 24, 1865.
20. Loc. Cit.

Bibliography

PRIMARY SOURCES

Barnes, Gilbert H., and Dwight L. Dumond, eds., Letters of *Theodore Dwight Weld, Agelina Grimke Weld and Sarah Grimke 1822-1844*, Peter Smith, Glouster, Mass., 1965.

Finch, Marianne, *An Englishwoman's Experience in America*, Negro University Press, New York, 1969.

Finney, Charles Grandison, *Lectures on Revivals of Religion*, Fleming H. Revell Co., New York, 1868.

Merrill, Walter, ed., *The Letters of William Lloyd Garrison, 1822-1835, Vols. I, II, and III*, Harvard University Press, Cambridge, 1971.

Tappan, Lewis, *Diary and Letters 1816-1839, 1844-1865, MSS*, Library of Congress, Washington, D.C.

Tappan, Lewis, *The Life of Arthur Tappan*, Negro Universities Press, Westport, Conn., 1970 (first edition, 1871).

Tocqueville, Alexis de, *Democracy in America*, Vol. I & II, Schocken Books, New York, 1961 (first edition, 1835).

OTHER SOURCES

Ahlstrom, Sydney E., *A Religious History of the American People*, Yale University Press, New Haven, 1972.

Baird, Robert, *Religion in the United States of America,* New York: Arno Press and the New York Times, 1969.

Barnes, Gilbert H., *The Anti-Slavery Impulse 1830-1844,* Harcourt, Brace Y World Inc., New York, 1933.

Billington, Ray Allen, *The Protestant Crusade, 1800-1860,* Quadrangle Books, Chicago, 1938.

Blassingame, John W., *The Slave Community: Plantation Life in the Antebellum South,* Oxford University Press, New York, 1972.

Cable, Mary and the editors of *American Heritage, American Manners & Morals,* American Heritage Publishing Company, Inc., New York, 1969.

Coit, Margaret L. and the editors of *Life, The Growing Years,* Vol. 3 of *The Life History of the United States,* Time, Inc., New York, 1963.

Davis, David Brion, *Antebellum Reform,* Harper and Row, New York, 1967.

Dwight, Henry Otis, *The Centennial History of the American Bible Society,* MacMillan Co., New York, 1916, Vol. 1.

Fish, Carl Russell, *The Rise of the Common Man 1830-1850,* (A History of American Life, Vol. VI), The MacMillan Co., New York, 1941.

Furnas, J.C., *The Americans: A Social History of the United States, 1587-1914,* G.P. Putnam's Sons, New York, 1969.

Grimke, Archibald H., *William Lloyd Garrison, The Abolitionist,* Negro Universities Press, New York, 1969.

Howse, Ernest Marshall, *Saints in Politics: The Clapham Sect and the Growth of Freedom,* University of Toronto Press, Toronto, 1952.

Ketchum, Richard M., *The World of George Washington,* American Heritage Publishing Company, New York, 1974.

Marsden, George M., *The Evangelical Mind and the New School Presbyterian Experience – A Case Study in Thought and Theology in Nineteenth Century America,* Yale University Press, New Haven, 1970.

Marty, Martin E., *Righteous Empire: The Protestant Experience in America,* Dial Press, New York, 1970.

Miller, John C., *The Colonial Image: Origens of American Culture,* George Braziller, New York, 1962.

Miller, Perry, *Nature's Nation,* Harvard University Press, Cambridge, 1967.

Miller, Perry, *The Transcendentalists, an Anthology,* Harvard University Press, Cambridge, 1950.

Morris, Richard B. and the editors of *Life, The Making of a Nation,* Vol. 2 of *The Life History of the United States,* Time, Inc., New York, 1963.

Nye, Russel Blaine, *The Cultural Life of the New Nation 1776-1830,* Harper & Brothers Publisher, New York, 1960.

Nye, Russell Blaine, *Society and Culture in America, 1830-1860,* Harper and Row Publishers, New York, 1974.

Orr, J. Edwin, *The Eager Feet: Evangelical Awakenings, 1790-1830.* Moody Press, Chicago, 1975.

Pessen, Edward, *Jacksonian America Society, Personality and Politics,* Dorsey Press, Homewood, Ill., 1969.

Riegel, Robert E., *Young America 1830-1840,* University of Oklahoma Press, Norman, Okla., 1949.

Schlesinger, Arthur M., Jr., *The Age of Jackson,* Little, Brown, & Company, Boston, Mass., 1945.

Smith, Timothy L., *Revivalism and Social Reform: American Protestantism on the Eve of the Civil War,* Abingdon Press, New York, 1957.

Thomas, Benjamin P., *Theodore Weld: Crusader for Freedom,* Rutgers University Press, New Brunswick, N.J., 1950.

Tyler, Alice Felt, *Freedom's Ferment: Phases of American Social History from the Colonial Period to the Outbreak of the Civil War,* Harper and Row Publishers, New York, 1944.

Weisberger, Bernard A., *They Gathered at the River: The Story of Revivalists and their Impact upon Religion in America,* Little, Brown, and Co., Boston, Mass., 1958.

Wyatt-Brown, Bertram, *Lewis Tappan and the Evangelical War Against Slavery,* The Press of Case Western Reserve University, Cleveland, Ohio, 1969.

Index